INVEST
LIKE AN AARDVARK

James M. Russo

First Edition Design Publishing
United States Canada London

Invest Like An Aardvark
Copyright ©2018 James M. Russo

ISBN 978-1506-907-47-5 HCJ
ISBN 978-1506-907-48-2 PBK
ISBN 978-1506-907-49-9 EBK

LCCN 2018963713

November 2018

Published and Distributed by
First Edition Design Publishing, Inc.
P.O. Box 17646, Sarasota, FL 34276-3217
www.firsteditiondesignpublishing.com

To my father who was the hardest working man I've ever known and the example to whom I owe the fortunate life I've lived.

Disclosures

This book includes candid statements and observations regarding investment strategies, individual securities, and economic and market conditions; however, there is no guarantee that these statements, opinions or forecasts will prove to be correct. These comments may also include the expression of opinions that are speculative in nature and should not be relied on as statements of fact. Altrius is committed to communicating with our investment partners as candidly as possible because we believe our investors benefit from understanding our investment philosophy and approach. Our views and opinions include "forward-looking statements" which may or may not be accurate over the long term. Forward-looking statements can be identified by words like "believe," "expect," "anticipate," or similar expressions. You should not place undue reliance on forward-looking statements, which are current as of the publication of this book. We disclaim any obligation to update or alter any forward-looking statements, whether as a result of new information, future events or otherwise. While we believe we have a reasonable basis for our appraisals and we have confidence in our opinions, actual results may differ materially from those we anticipate.

The information provided in this material should not be considered a recommendation to buy, sell or hold any particular security. The S&P 500˙ Index is an unmanaged index of 500 selected common stocks, most of which are listed on the New York Stock Exchange. The Index is adjusted for dividends, weighted towards stocks with large market capitalizations and represents approximately two-thirds of the total market value of all domestic common stocks. The Russell 3000 Value Index is an unmanaged index commonly used as a benchmark to measure value manager performance and characteristics. The Dow Jones U.S. Select Dividend Index is an unmanaged index commonly used as a benchmark to measure dividend manager performance and characteristics. The Russell 2000 Index, the Russell 2000 Growth Index, and the Russell 2000 Value Index are unmanaged indices commonly used as benchmarks to measure small cap manager performance and characteristics. The MSCI EAFE® Index is a free float-adjusted market capitalization index that is designed to measure developed market equity performance, excluding the U.S. & Canada. The Bloomberg Barclays U.S. Aggregate Bond Index and Bank of America Merrill Lynch US High Yield Master II Total Return Index are unmanaged indices that are commonly used as benchmarks to measure fixed income performance and characteristics. Index performance returns do not reflect any management fees, transaction costs or expenses. Investments cannot be made directly in an index. **Investments made with Altrius Capital Management, Inc. are not deposits or obligations of any bank, are not guaranteed by any bank, are not insured by the FDIC or any other agency, and involve investment risks, including possible loss of the principal amount invested. Past performance is not a guarantee of future returns.**

Acknowledgements

To my wife Annie, thank you for regularly supporting my 70- to 80-hour work weeks and enduring more during the year-long endeavor of writing this book. You are not only my partner in life and work, but also my closest confidant, and whom I continually rely on for a sounding board, and whose opinion I hold so dear. Without your love, support, and tireless devotion to our family, my life's work and this book would not be possible—nor would our children find their way to school clothed and well fed.

To my children Hannah, Maximus, Augustus, and Elena, for your unending inspiration—and sometimes exasperation. I believe being a parent is one of life's most important, thankless, and difficult of jobs. As I often believe you are too young, or too disinterested in listening to my economic and financial planning lectures (among discourses on other topics), I sometimes found myself writing this book to you in an attempt to leave these lessons with you when you are ready to accept them—or at least intelligently argue against their merits. I hope you find some time one day to dust off this book and read it, then share it with my grandchildren as my legacy to them.

To Rob, for taking the time to write the Foreword, for your very kind remarks and for not including all of my faults and imperfections you've tolerated for the three plus decades in which we've remained the best of friends. I deeply appreciate your wit, scholar, and example, but most of all your friendship.

To Brady Gingrich, for your meticulous proofreading, assistance with and production of charts and grammatical excellence. You are simply the best intern I have ever employed and one of the finest young men and minds that I know. Your intellectual curiosity and work ethic will serve you well in life and I hope someday you will work permanently with our firm after gleaning travel, ideas and experience from my larger financial competitors. Enjoy your 20's with those firms so you will better appreciate the benefits of working for a benevolent dictator boss and boutique investment management firm in which you may affect change, drive results, and find value. Alternatively, I'd also be happy to employ you directly upon graduation from UNC/business school (or right now) due to your maturity and current worth.

To Michael Dubes, for putting up with my obsessive-compulsive disorder and dyslexia (though fortunately mild). Your brainstorming, editorial expertise and patience with my anxieties and inexperience made this book possible.

INVEST
LIKE AN AARDVARK

James M. Russo

Table of Contents

Foreword

I first met Jim Russo as a teenager playing pickup basketball in New Jersey, where we both grew up. Jim was a regular fixture on the local courts and we played a lot together, beginning a friendship that has lasted nearly 35 years.

While Jim was a talented basketball player and gifted athlete, it was other things that made him different. He was a natural leader: confident, determined, fair and generous. When Jim was on the court, the games would often revolve around him, with the rest of us looking to Jim for direction, for what would happen next. Jim had clear vision, understood the game and made good decisions. He always seemed to make the right pass; always knew where the ball should go. It was typically better to be playing with Jim than against him.

The vision, judgment, decisiveness and determination that Jim displayed back then have all been evident in the years that followed. Those same qualities led to his success at the United States Naval Academy, honorable service as a pilot in the Marine Corps and ultimately to the founding of his investment firm.

Today, Jim applies the same confidence, decisiveness and independent thinking in his professional life. His energy, focus and commitment to seeing things through to a successful conclusion are invaluable when making long-term investment decisions on behalf of clients. Like most intelligent and driven people, Jim has strong opinions, especially when it comes to investing. Jim is fiercely independent and has never followed the crowd; a trait reflected in his approach to investing and on clear display in this book.

Jim didn't take the usual path to the investment business. He started his firm from the ground up, away from conventional thinking and conflict, obligated to do only what was right for his clients. The outstanding investment performance he has generated for clients over the past two decades is a testament that approach.

Throughout the time that I have known him, Jim has always been willing to challenge himself, others and, in particular, the ordinary way of thinking.

That's what Jim is doing with this book. He's challenging conventional thinking and, most importantly, challenging us to think differently about investing. So, take the challenge. Read the book. Think for yourself and form your own ideas. Invest wisely.

Robert MacDonnell, JD/MBA

Prologue

Like me, the aardvark is big, slow and a bit ugly. He's not a big game hunter. He's not hunting for high flying stocks. He eats the easily foraged food, like ants. What ants are to the aardvark, dividends are to our firm. They are the easily scavenged returns. The aardvark hunts at night, alone and unafraid. He's contrarian by nature and is completely unique as the only living creature in his scientific classification order. There's no other animal quite like him. He has giant ears, which he keeps raised to be mindful of what might go wrong while he is searching for dividends. He has big sharp claws, ideal for digging deep to uncover value. He works well into the night and is diligent in his search. I think the aardvark is a pretty cool animal and accurately reflects who we are as an investment firm. A mainstream Wall Street firm we are not.

Introduction

I was born in Paterson, New Jersey and grew up during the 70's and 80's in Wayne—a town about 20 miles outside of New York City. I am the first child of a Polish mother and Italian father who was the hardest working man I've ever known and the example to whom I owe the fortunate life I've lived.

My grandfather presented my father with a steady job collecting tolls for the state, but "Pop" decided to go to Atlas Barber School in New York City to attain his barber's license. My father spent 13 years building his clientele in Paterson, but business was getting difficult during the late 60's and early 70's as the Beatles ushered in longer hair styles and he felt he needed to find other opportunities. Applying for a job as a broker and insurance salesman, he had to explain to my mom how he was declined for a job paying commissions only. Going back for another interview, he convinced his future boss to give him a shot and subsequently spent the majority of his thirty-year career as the top broker in his branch until his retirement at age 62. The road was difficult as he began his career during the economic stagflation of the 1973-1975 recession. He supplemented the sale of insurance and financial products by cutting hair and tending bar at night; however, he never wavered in his resolve to take care of his family.

Not a day goes by that I don't recall with gratitude the many lessons he taught me. Sacrificing his entire life for our family, he died just a year after retiring at age 63, succumbing to lung cancer in 2005. He remains the most influential person in my life.

My work ethic and entrepreneurial spirit are the direct result of his efforts. Twenty years after founding my investment firm, Altrius Capital Management, I still work seventy hour weeks and wake up every day with the same excitement I felt two decades ago.

Though much of my early life through my late twenties entailed serious consideration of a calling to the priesthood (and even work towards a Master of Arts in Religious Studies at St. Joseph's Seminary), my primary ambition as a young man was to attend Notre Dame University and then Columbia Law School. That was the grand plan growing up in the shadow of New York, where it was common for young men to aspire to become attorneys.

My life instead took a dramatically different direction when I decided I wanted to fly airplanes and serve my country. I received and accepted an appointment to attend the U. S. Naval Academy and graduated with a degree in Economics and was commissioned a Second Lieutenant in the Marine Corps. I served the subsequent eight years flying all over the world, ultimately piloting the KC-130 Hercules.

Often, our experiences have a profound impact on our lives that isn't immediately apparent. My experiences flying everything from basic transport assignments to more dangerous evacuations and search and rescue refueling missions helped instill a respect for following certain principles and training in advance for what could go wrong. Among pilots, we used to say that the Naval Air Training and Operating Procedures (NATOPS) were written in blood. As in flying, remaining disciplined in your investment process can keep your portfolio from being killed. Living to fight another day and remaining humble is critical to investment success over the long term. More about this later.

My far-flung travels as a Marine pilot also help shape my approach to investing. Unlike most of my Wall Street contemporaries, who tend to see the world as comprised of New York, San Francisco and Hong Kong, my perspective is much more inclusive in nature, both globally and domestically.

My military missions would range from one or two weeks to much longer stays flying missions overseas. Whether in Europe, Asia or Africa, my travel allowed me to see how the local economies functioned in different areas of the world. It gave me a global perspective that served me well in later years as an investor. I believe it afforded me a distinct advantage over my Wall Street friends who typically attended Ivy League universities, went on to attain MBAs and settled into working in Manhattan, where they formed more constrained views of the economy and investing. It became their permanent assessment; you can hear it in the way they talk. It's extremely localized, reflecting whatever is impacting New York at the time. They tend to lack a global economic understanding. Indeed, they don't have much of an American perspective, that is, how the economy outside of New York actually works, and are often swayed by prevalent sentiment or market momentum.

I believe in a broader approach. As I often remark during our investment committee meetings when news events drive sentiment: "What impact does this have on how many hamburgers are eaten in China, chocolate consumed in Latin America or soft drinks in Africa?"

In addition to my global travels, taking me through Asia, Europe, north of the Arctic circle in Bodø, Norway and south of the equator in Congo, Africa, I've been to 44 of the 50 states in the U.S. Traveling through small towns in

Kentucky, Kansas, Louisiana, and North Dakota, gives one a unique perspective, with each having their own local economy, many of them vibrant.

In addition to our firm's office in New Jersey, we have offices in North Carolina, where I founded the firm in 1997, while I was still actively serving in the Marine Corps. New Bern, NC has a population of about 30,000 people and contains hospitals, medical and dental practices, real estate firms, restaurants, and supermarkets. We have private clients ranging from firms that sell tires and repair automobiles to a chemical company that supplies companies all over the world with flavorings generating over millions in annual revenue. New Bern — and small-town America for that matter — is not a large money center driving billion dollar firms. However, there are small loans being made every day; five hundred thousand or a million for small businesses to build their business in their community — which adds up on a global macro scale. It is from small-town business owners, physicians, and retirees who moved to rural America that our business grew.

The combination of hundreds of thousands of local economies like New Bern — both domestically and abroad — make up the true global economy that looks and functions remarkably different from that of New York. Having lived most of the past thirty years in small southern towns before moving back to the New York City area, one gets quite a different feel for how the economy works than someone living in metro New York and working on Wall Street. The closer you get to Wall Street, the more that difference becomes apparent.

Facing clients across the table who have entrusted us with their life savings has had a dramatic impact on me and our investment process since the firm's founding. My friends who look down on Central Park from their offices in New York City, rarely if ever meet face to face with their client investors. They are disconnected from their clients, whose portfolios don't receive the attention and care necessary for proper management.

I live and work with many of these people, some of whom are close friends. They went to top colleges, landed jobs with large investment firms as analysts, commute to the city and back, and along the way inherit a Wall Street mentality. I saw the mistakes these money managers made during the late 1990's and early 2000's. It motivated me to find a way to better manage risk and provide income for our clients by focusing on value and dividends. We were also able to save our clients' money by stripping out the additional layer of mutual fund expenses.

I founded Altrius Capital Management in 1997 and have always had to look across the table at my clients, realizing they have entrusted me with their life savings. I invest side by side with them in the same U.S. stocks, international companies, and bonds owned by my clients. By eating what I cook, owning the same companies I research, I believe our interests are more aligned and that we experience together the same fears arisen by market volatility while driving toward the same end of investment success. We will certainly stumble at times along the way. However, this journey is a lengthy trek and investment success a long-distance race.

Section I

Avoid Being Killed on the Dangerous Savanna

CHAPTER ONE

Managing Risk

Live to Fight Another Day

A client recently sent me an email lamenting the fact that he hadn't bought Amazon stock years ago. It sometimes frustrates me that despite so much evidence to the contrary, not to mention my 20 plus years of advising investors to beware of stocks with unreasonable multiples, so many people continue to chase high-flying stocks.

Wall Street loves sexy, high-priced stocks like Amazon, Tesla, and Netflix. They're easy for brokers to sell because investors fear missing out on the next big thing so they take big risks. But Wall Street — and investors who follow the advice of Wall Street brokerage firms — continually gets it backwards. They should be taking less risk rather than investing in the tantalizing.

Investors should be buying boring, more stable stocks that pay a growing and above average dividend yield. They would enjoy less volatility, and potentially enjoy better performance over time. They would avoid investing in what I call hope. When you buy a stock like Amazon trading at a ridiculous multiple like 100 times earnings, you're buying the hope that it will continue to grow at an outlandish rate. It is of course possible, and does happen at times, but don't bet on it.

I've never been part of the Wall Street mentality. I've never interviewed for a position with a Wall Street firm. I never went down the traditional Wall Street path of acquiring an MBA, then going to work at a major brokerage firm or investment bank.

I went to the Naval Academy, flew airplanes in the Marine Corps for eight years, then founded my company, Altrius Capital Management. Managing risk from the cockpit of an airplane is not unlike managing portfolio risk. You learn that there are things you shouldn't do if you want to survive. While there are people smarter than me working on Wall Street, a lot of them have blown up their portfolios, hedge funds, and money management firms because they did something they shouldn't do: they took too much risk and didn't live to fight another day.

High profile fund managers like Ken Heebner, frequently cited as a stock-picking genius, saw his 5 Star rating collapse to 1 Star. His CGM Focus Fund gained just 0.25% annually over the trailing decade through December 31, 2017, trailing the S&P 500 by an average 8.25 percentage points a year according to Morningstar. In 2010, Morningstar named Bruce Berkowitz a *Fund Manager of the Decade*; yet, his Fairholme Fund lost 32.42% during 2011. His fund has subsequently ranked among the worst performing funds over the past decade, trailing his peers by more than 3% on an annual basis. It tumbled from almost $19 billion to less than $2 billion due to massive concentrations in certain stocks and sectors.[1] Bill Miller was touted as the smartest guy on the planet for beating the S&P 500 for fifteen years in a row. His undoing was a period of 7 or 8 years where the fund underperformed terribly because of large bets in certain sectors.

High-flying hedge fund managers have suffered similar fates. Julian Robertson's Tiger Management Corp, which managed over $20 billion in assets through the late 1990's, was followed by a precipitous spiral of investor withdrawals and poor performance ending with the fund's closing in 2000. Amaranth Advisors peaked at $9 billion in assets under management before collapsing in September 2006 after losing over $5 billion on natural gas futures. Atticus Capital, founded by Timothy Barakett and one of the largest hedge funds in the world in 2007 with $20 billion in assets under management, suffered steep losses and returned money to investors by 2009. Satellite Asset Management, run by three veterans of Soros Fund Management and with approximately $7 billion at its peak, hemorrhaged assets during the financial crisis only to join the hedge fund graveyard of 2008.

All of these managers took too much risk. These are exceptionally smart people who were presumably making intelligent decisions for their clients. However, their fatal flaw was in using leverage or taking huge positions in individual securities or sectors which led to their ultimate demise. Each clearly lacked what I believe to be one of the most important characteristics of an investment manager — humility. Remaining humble and continually considering where one might be wrong is critical to managing risk and long term survival.

I don't recommend you emulate the mistakes of these failed managers chasing fast returns. Slow and steady wins the race. You don't want to be overly concentrated in one sector or asset class. It's important to ensure your portfolio is sufficiently concentrated to impact performance, but also adequately diversified to manage risk. Diversifying your portfolio is the only free lunch you get.

> *"Simplicity is the ultimate sophistication."*
> Leonardo daVinci

I consider it my responsibility to try to alleviate worry for our clients. Obviously, it's not always possible to do this, but I try to provide leadership and prevent them from panic when times are difficult. I recall a client who wanted to vacate the market during the financial crisis of 2008. We sat down and went through his portfolio stock by stock. I told him "Pepsi is still paying you a dividend and I believe they will continue to do so. Do you want to sell Pepsi? How about Unilever, Pfizer or Microsoft, which are paying dividends with yields over 5%? Even though they're down in value right now, they're still paying you a dividend." He wisely agreed to stay invested, collecting his dividends and patiently waiting for his portfolio to eventually recover in value.

In addition to humility, I believe a portfolio manager should have what my ninth grade religion teacher at Seton Hall Prep described as *sticktuitiveness*. While extolling character virtues to fortify one for life, Fr. Kilcarr counseled us on the importance of dogged persistence. I believe that not getting scared out of stocks during times of market tumult and displaying the fortitude to remain invested long term is critical to long-term success. As in my flying days, investing is similar in that you should be prepared for turbulence along the route, but if buffeting winds cause you to panic and parachute out of the plane, you certainly won't reach your destination. We cannot control the weather, but we can plan for uncertainties and stick to our flight plan because it assures the best chance of safely reaching our target. Investing in the stocks of sound, dividend-paying companies can help alleviate the mistake of selling when a stock's value is lower. The reason is you are still being paid a dividend to be patient.

Peter Lynch, author of his insightful books "One Up On Wall Street" and "Beating the Street" wrote that "stocks are not lottery tickets; there are companies behind them you don't need to rush." He has also stated (as I firmly believe) that "the key organ in your body is your stomach, not your brain. It's always going to be scary, there's always going to be something to worry about, and you just have to forget about all of that. If you own good companies, you'll do well."

The same discipline is true when markets or companies are selling at excessive valuations and greed can lure investors to invest in companies they should not. While Warren Buffett admits having missed opportunities on Amazon and Google, he has coined some fascinating analogies between investing and baseball:

> *"The stock market is a no-called-strike game. You don't have to swing at everything. You can wait for your pitch. The problem when you're a money manager is that your fans keep yelling, 'swing, you bum!'"*

> *"In his book, 'The Science of Hitting,' Ted Williams notes that the most important thing for a hitter is to wait for the right pitch. And that's exactly the philosophy I have about investing: Wait for the right pitch and wait for the right deal. And it will come…it's the key to investing."*

> *"What's nice about investing is you don't have to swing at pitches. You can wait for the pitch you want. In investing, just as in baseball, to put runs on the scoreboard one must watch the playing field, not the scoreboard."*

> *"I've never swung at a ball while it's still in the pitcher's glove."*

Buffett doesn't buy startup companies or those without a long history of stable earnings. Like Buffett, I prefer to invest with a margin of safety when purchasing a company by not paying too much. When you buy a stock, it's important to think like a business owner — which you are when you own a stock. I would add the caveat of wanting to be *paid to wait* when purchasing a company, preferring those that pay dividends, which is like paying yourself a salary while waiting for the company to achieve full value over the long term.

Wall Street tends to do just the opposite and rarely thinks in terms of buying a business. They should be looking at buying a stock in the same manner as purchasing a car dealership or Subway franchise. Instead, they look at a stock as something to buy in the morning, sell in the afternoon, then buy again in the evening.

That's why the dividend component is so important. It better aligns your interests with those of the companies that are committed to paying you. It's as if you bought that car dealership and the dividend is your salary for running the company. That dividend is going to be there for you if you run an efficient business. The valuation of that business is going to fluctuate based on how people feel about the company, but the intrinsic value of the business will be intact, as will the dividend that pays you for being an owner assuming you run a profitable business.

The scarcity of value investors on Wall Street can be attributed to the fact that being a value investor requires thinking unconventionally, and Wall Street has always been focused on growth and new ideas. It's largely composed of young MBAs who aren't old enough to remember the last recession or bear market. Many can enjoy profitable careers as analysts chasing trends and momentum strategies. Few get blamed for chasing hot stocks, simply believing the market moved against them, or are quickly replaced by the next batch of young professionals chasing the next best thing to catch the Street's attention. In contrast, value investing by nature entails periods of underperformance which can lead investors or investment firms to fire you for missing the hot sector.

Lower beta, dividend paying stocks selling at attractive or reasonable valuations are boringly beautiful to me. They are the true sexy stocks. When we purchased McDonald's at the end of 2013, Wall Street and most investors believed the company's best days were behind it and instead desired to focus on sexier, expensive growth companies such as Chipotle, which today still doesn't pay a dividend. The results proved me correct. McDonald's steadily grew its dividend, enabling us to be paid to wait during its turnaround. While we owned the company, McDonald's grew its earnings and well outperformed Chipotle.

Disciplined value investing with dividends has always been and will continue to be at the heart of my investment process, even when I am outperformed by a particular index or sexy security. That's because I believe absolute return is more important than relative performance. Providing sound risk-adjusted returns is superior than attempting to shoot the stars out investing in the next great idea like Amazon or Shake Shack. Though I prefer Shake Shack's burgers to McDonald's, it's important not confuse a particular product with a company and to only invest in companies in which the price paid is reasonable for the potential growth.

It's why, unlike Wall Street, I eschew high-flying fad stocks and momentum investing in favor of investing like our mascot, the aardvark.

"Wall Street is the only place that people ride to in a Rolls Royce to get advice from those who take the subway."
Warren Buffett

CHAPTER TWO

Emotional Investing

Not Keeping your Head Will Get You Killed

The annual study titled "Quantitative Analysis of Investor Behavior" by financial research firm Dalbar concluded that during 2016, the average equity mutual fund investor underperformed the S&P 500 by a wide margin of 4.70%. The broader market gained 11.96% while the average equity investor earned just 7.26%. During the same year, the average fixed income mutual fund investor underperformed the Bloomberg Barclay's Aggregate Bond Index by 1.42%.

This was not an anomaly. The 20-year annualized return for the average equity fund investor was 4.79% compared to 7.68% for the S&P 500.

The performance discrepancy flies in the face of the efficient market hypothesis (EMH), a conventional view that the markets operate efficiently and investors act rationally. The burgeoning field of behavioral finance holds the contradictory opinion that people tend to act irrationally when making investment decisions.

The concept of behavioral finance has been around for over a century but arguably it became relevant in 1979 with the publication of Daniel Kahneman and Amos Tversky's abstract, "A Study of Decision Making Under Risk." It concluded that rather than calculating the universe of potential outcomes and selecting the optimal one, investors calculate outcomes against a subjective reference point, such as the purchase price of a stock. Moreover, investors are loss averse, which means they are willing to take on more risk in the face of losses, but become more afraid of risk when it comes to protecting their gains.[2]

The psychological aspects of behavioral finance explore the role cognitive biases play in decision making. Cognitive biases are the instinctive leaps our

17

minds make — our gut reactions and things we believe we know although we're not sure how we know them. Scientists believe they are a relic of evolution; little shortcuts programmed into our minds to help us process faster. But they sometimes lead us just as quickly to the wrong conclusions.[3]

Many of these innate biases contribute to the irrationality displayed by people making investment choices. Some of the more common — and potentially most detrimental — biases include anchoring, confirmation, and herding.

"The investor's chief problem — and even his worst enemy — is likely to be himself."
Benjamin Graham

Anchoring Bias

When you rely on an initial piece of information to make subsequent judgments, you're succumbing to anchoring bias. Psychologists use the term to describe the human tendency to rely too heavily, or anchor, on a single piece of information when making decisions.

This anchoring bias impacts many financial decisions. The awards from lawsuits are influenced by the plaintiff's initial demand — the plaintiff gets more by requesting more. In real estate, people are unconsciously influenced by arbitrary posted prices. In online auctions, the prices bid are anchored by the non-binding "buy-now price." Earnings forecasts by financial analysts are biased towards the previous months' data as an anchor.[4]

Let's assume an investor has a million dollars in assets tied up in just one or two stocks and the value plummets by 30 or 40%. What I often see people do is tenaciously cling to those stocks, waiting for their values to return to their original worth. They refuse to sell, regardless of how long it takes. They are anchored to the higher value of those stocks. Similarly, when real estate prices drop, homeowners will refuse to sell their depressed properties until values return to previous highs or what they originally paid. This happens even when the homeowner is not underwater on the property.

I sometimes use an analogy to help clients abandon their anchoring bias. I ask if they were sitting on the cash equivalent of the diminished value of a declined stock, would they take that cash and reinvest it into that security? If the answer is no, which it almost always is, I ask, "Then why are you sitting on this investment? Learn your lesson, cut your losses, understand that it was a mistake, and properly diversify your portfolio going forward. Don't make that mistake again."

As a financial advisor, if I suggested to someone with a million dollars to invest it all into a single stock, they would probably look at me like I was crazy. They might comment, "Jim, you're a nice guy with a good track record and you seem to have built up a good business, but that's the dumbest thing I've ever heard."

However, that's exactly what investors do when they have a large percentage of their portfolio invested in a single stock and refuse to sell any of it.

In his best-selling book on cognitive biases and heuristics, "Thinking Fast & Slow," Daniel Kahneman, professor of behavioral & cognitive psychology at Princeton University, offers this example of anchoring: "In negotiation, many people think that you have an advantage if you go second. But actually, the advantage is going first. And the reason is in something about the way the mind works. The mind tries to make sense out of whatever you put before it. This built-in tendency that we have of trying to make sense of everything that we encounter, is a mechanism for anchoring."

Good advice from Kahneman's book: "If you've had 10,000 hours of training in a predictable, rapid-feedback environment — chess, firefighting, anesthesiology — then blink. In all other cases, think."

An Anchoring Story

An unfortunate experience I had with a client occurred early in my career during the dot.com bubble. A husband and wife had separate investment accounts, each with all of their money invested in their employer's stock — his with Sprint, hers with Quintiles Transnational.

I advised them to diversify, which the husband reluctantly agreed to do, allowing me to sell all of his Sprint stock in 1999. At year's end, the couple called and were angry with me for suggesting they sell the stock. The reason? Sprint was up approximately 55% for the year, peaking at 64.68 in October, but the husband's newly-diversified portfolio was up *only* 28%. Their anger subsequently abated when Sprint stock imploded the following year, nosediving to 17.68 in December, 2000. It continued its downward spiral, temporarily bottoming out at 8.50 in July, 2002. The husband later thanked me because he realized had he not followed my advice and sold the stock, his $500,000 nest egg would have shriveled to a fraction of its value.

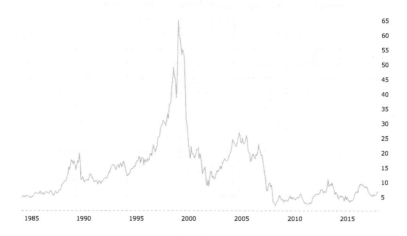

Fig. 2.1: Sprint Stock History

Meanwhile, the wife, who worked for many years at Quintiles Transnational, accumulated $1.5 million of that company's stock. Quintiles was another of the dot.com era's high flyers. I offered the wife the same advice — liquidate all of your stock and diversify as we did with your husband's Sprint stock. She refused: "I think it's going to go up a little more, probably to 1.8 or 2 million. I'll sell it then."

Then never happened. The stock took a precipitous drop from its 64.68 high to just 17.85 over the following 14 months. It continued to sink and was down to 8.5 by July, 2002. The company that looked so good on paper turned out to be cooking its books, causing the stock to implode.

The wife's $1.5 million in stock shrunk to a value of approximately $300,000. She still refused to sell. She was anchored on the $1.5 million she was certain the stock would eventually be worth and could not bring herself to accept the loss and move on. She would still own that stock today had the original founder of the company not decided to buy it back at $14.50 and take it private in 2003.[5]

When that happened, she was incredulous. I told her, "It's not going any higher; $14.50 a share is what he's buying it back for and that's all you will get. You and your husband will either have to continue working or retire and live on $800,000: your $300,000 and his $500,000. You're in your 50's. Work another 10 years or accept that you're going to have to spend less."

Greed can cause people to do stupid things. Here's a case where one day, a couple is hollering at me because their portfolio is only up 28% for the year; a few months later, the husband is contrite and thankful I got him out of the stock he was so attached to; and finally, the wife is living in disbelief because she is anchored to a stock value that blew up and no longer has any relevance.

Anchoring can cause investors to fall in love with stocks. Unfortunately, stocks don't always love them back.

"Now is always the hardest time to invest."
Bernard Baruch

Confirmation Bias

Confirmation is a behavioral bias that prompts you to embrace information that supports what you already believe and ignore information that refutes your beliefs. Confirmation bias occurs when people filter out potentially useful facts and opinions that don't coincide with their preconceived notions.[6]

While we like to imagine that our beliefs are rational, logical, and objective, the fact is that our ideas are often based on paying attention to the information that upholds our ideas. Confirmation biases impact how we gather information, but they also influence how we interpret and recall information. For example, people who support or oppose a particular issue will not only seek information to support it, they will also interpret news stories in a way that upholds their existing ideas.[7] Having our beliefs confirmed makes us feel validated whereas conflicting information might make us feel insecure or foolish.

Oftentimes, it happens when we attach an emphasis to the outcomes we desire, such as investing too much in the stock of the company we work for, which also reduces diversification.[8]

Confirmation Story

A marvelous example of confirmation bias comes from leadership coach Robert Dickman.

> *I was involved in a film which was cast here in the United States but would be shooting in a foreign country. Many young leading actresses auditioned for the female lead however the director was immediately smitten by one actresses' reading. The casting director and*

producers did not feel she was right for the role and challenged the director's decision. The director however would only hear from people who confirmed his casting decision. He countered that she had real talent that no one else was seeing, reminding us how easily she was able to cry in the scene, and she was eventually cast.

On the first day of filming outside of the United States, it became clear that she was indeed able to cry easily, she couldn't act her way out of a paper bag. After being fired, she shed real tears. The director's confirmation bias caused a broken-hearted actress and added tens of thousands of dollars in production costs.[9]

Confirmation and Excessive Trading

Terrance Odean, Professor of Finance at UC Berkeley, co-authored a brilliant paper titled "Trading is Hazardous to Your Wealth."[10] One of the conclusions of the article was the dramatic empirical evidence that overconfidence (a form of confirmation bias) leads to excessive trading, which results in diminished investment performance.

An analogy I use about trading being hazardous to your wealth relates to flying. Fighter pilots are trained to take immediate actions in emergencies. If they have an engine failure, the first thing they are trained to do is execute a certain set of procedures to try to get the engine restarted. If after some initial attempts, the engine doesn't re-start (particularly when the ground is quickly approaching), they eject.

In flight school, we were ingrained with these procedures. We drilled and drilled so they became second nature. In times of crisis, you may be paralyzed by fear and incapable of rational thinking, but your training takes over and you respond automatically. If you train properly and rely on your experience, you won't do anything stupid.

Training for KC-130 pilots differs from initial flight training as the aircraft is not equipped with ejection seats. Thus, we Marine KC-130 pilots used to joke that the first procedure for an emergency is to "sit on your hands and think," meaning don't touch anything. Don't do anything stupid in the heat of the moment.

Investors frequently do something stupid in the heat of the moment or when they are frightened. There is always a reason for investor anxiety: presidential elections, terrorist attacks, Brexit, government shutdowns, Bird flu, Y2K, wars, the list is endless. While the pundits claim to know what these events mean, the truth is that no one knows for certain how the economy and investors will react to any of these events in the short term.

Twenty five years later, I still recall my flight training and our *unofficial* emergency procedure to sit on your hands. Investors should embrace a similar procedure: sit on your hands rather than haphazardly trading in response to the day's news. Don't sell stock in Pepsi due to some event a newscaster or pundit stated was critical. Sit on your hands and first consider whether the crisis of the day has any bearing on the number of Pepsi's consumed in India. If the answer is no, you shouldn't be trading.

Herd Mentality

Herding occurs when we allow collective behavior to override our personal instincts. The combined actions of a large group convince us they must know something we don't. We assume they have better information than we do. Those susceptible to the herding bias make investment decisions they would not make as informed individuals.

Reading a clinical definition of herding is nothing like the experience of seeing it in action. There is great peer pressure to join the crowd — typically, those chasing the latest investment fad. How could so many people be wrong?

There is abundant empirical evidence of the dangers of merging with the mob, from the crash of 1929 to the dot.com bubble burst in 2000 to the real estate debacle of 2008. One must assume that investors are aware of these cataclysmic events, but they choose to ignore the lessons of history, believing instead that, "this time it's different."

It's not.

Herding is usually characterized by excessive, short-term trading, and momentum strategies. Wall Street product marketers are well aware of the herding mentality. This week, I received a solicitation for some newly-minted 3X leveraged exchange traded notes (ETNs) based on the FANG+™ Index, which includes the currently hot growth stocks: Facebook, Amazon, Netflix, and Google.

Marketers know that investors dread being left out of the latest trend and are prime candidates for virtually any new investment product that mimics the latest fad stampede.

An interesting take on herding behavior comes from quora.com. "If we hold a different opinion from the rest of the group the anterior cingulate cortex, also called the *oops* area of the brain, produces an error signal. In order to try and fix that error signal, we modify our opinion to the opinion of the rest of the group, even if we think that the opinion of theirs is wrong."

Be a Brave Contrarian

Better to be like the aardvark. He's not out there in the hot sun with the rest of the crowd, blindly hunting the next hot stock. He has the courage to go out alone at night and hunt the easy food while being alert to what can go wrong.

Like the first unofficial procedure for a KC-130 pilot in an emergency, you have to resist the urge to "do something" when market volatility occurs. In my experience, women tend to be better investors than men because they tend to think longer term and don't have the strong "fight or flight" genetic predisposition. Men are driven to act, to "do something" and start trading, thereby becoming the hazard to their wealth that Professor Odean identified.

Appearing on a morning news show in 2017, Warren Buffett expressed the opinion that when it comes to investing, having high intelligence is not what matters most; it's your emotional stability.

Emotional stability when investing is not a new occurrence. Sir Isaac Newton, one of the world's greatest mathematicians and physicists, heavily invested in the South Sea Company, one of best-performing stocks in England at the time. The stock experienced a meteoric eightfold rise in less than six months, and while Newton didn't time the rise all that well, he still managed to doubled his money, selling his stock and pocketing a handsome 7,000-pound profit.

As the shares of South Sea continued their upward journey, Newton, one of history's most brilliant minds, couldn't control his emotions. Like any other gullible investor, he was swept up in the wild enthusiasm and jumped back into the stock at a much higher price. Like the tulip craze, the bubble burst on South Sea Company and the stock plunged, losing more than 80% of its value. It left Newton with a loss of some 20,000 pounds, roughly three million in today's value.

Speaking later about his poor judgment, Newton confessed that he could calculate the emotions of heavenly bodies but not the madness of the mob. Inconsolable after the incident, Newton forbade anyone to speak the words *South Sea* in his presence for the rest of his life.

If Newton were alive today, he might be tempted to follow the crowd and buy into Bitcoin. When my Uber driver gave me a tip to buy Bitcoin, I knew the madness of the mob had once again descended upon us.

After a few clients called to ask about it, I advised them that anyone who bets on Bitcoin, or any other cryptocurrency, is rampantly speculating rather than investing. Not only is it a fad, it's the worst kind of fad because unlike a stock, there is absolutely no way to fundamentally judge the intrinsic value of Bitcoin as it produces no cash flow nor has it any earnings. As such, it's impossible to make a determination when to buy or sell it. Even if I could make a judgement on Bitcoin, it's unlikely I would do so as my firm instead focuses on investing our clients' hard-earned money in stocks and bonds which produce immediate income through dividends and interest and sell at reasonable or undervalued prices.

The Successful Investor

The exponential rise of Bitcoin and other cryptocurrencies triggers investors' emotions and behavioral biases. On the flip side, it offers us aardvark investors an opportunity to restate some of the core principles and practices that underlie our investment approach.

Successful long-term investors are disciplined and patient. They are honest about what they know, don't know, or can't know (the unknowable).

Successful investors have the humility to know not every decision will turn out to be right and that simply having conviction about something doesn't mean it will happen as they expect.

Successful investors are willing to challenge their own ideas and admit when they are wrong — whether due to new information and changing circumstances or an error in their original thesis. They keep their eyes on their long-term financial objectives and on the underlying fundamentals that ultimately drive investment returns.

Successful investors don't get emotionally involved in the day-to-day noise of the financial news channels or the zigs and zags of the markets. If the market isn't presenting them with compelling investment opportunities, they are content to hold their current positions. In other words, they don't confuse activity with progress. Charlie Munger calls it "sit on your ass investing."

CHAPTER THREE

Market Timing

You Won't Eat if You Don't Hunt

Advisors with significant assets under management get recurring visitors: wholesalers from the big mutual fund companies, pitching their latest hot product. It can be an irresistible temptation for advisors to simply go with the flow and recommend whatever is popular — and consequently easier to sell — to their clients. Usually, these are funds or alternatives that mimic existing products already selling well, sometimes with an added twist or tweak to make them just a bit sexier.

You might expect advisors to be smarter than the average investor — particularly over the long term — but in my experience, many are not.

Case in point: We recently received a redemption notice from an advisor whose client needed cash. Because the high yield bond market had sold off a "whopping" 1%, it became the first asset he chose to liquidate to raise the cash. This is the kind of misguided thinking you might expect from an uninformed investor, not a presumably knowledgeable financial advisor. Yet these kinds of overreactions happen with regularity among those who call themselves professional investment advisors.

I refer to them as herd advisors. They tend to move their clients in and out of the market in response to volatility or short-term events. Whether they are too timid to prevent their clients from doing something imprudent, or simply don't know better themselves, they display the same type of emotional decision-making rampant among individual investors.

It's evidently difficult for advisors to resist following the herd when making investment recommendations. During the tech bubble, the mutual fund complex was pumping out internet and tech funds as fast as they could think up names for them. Advisors bought them hand over fist for their clients...right up to the time when they collapsed. Then the real estate bubble came along and what did advisors do? They bought real estate funds and REITs as fast as the mutual fund companies could push them out the door. A sector heats up and the whole Wall Street manufacturing apparatus goes into high gear. Like a contractor spewing foam insulation, fund manufacturers fill every nook and cranny of the advisor's arsenal with the newest iteration. The excitement continues until the last fool buys in and the folly finally ends. Angry investors fire their advisors, who deserve their termination for not having more wisdom or courage. Meanwhile, the mutual fund complex goes back to the drawing board and creates the next "can't miss" product.

Like a pinball machine ball, herd advisors bounce their clients from one hazard to the next, most of it based on whatever the financial product producers have decided is the next "standing room only" production. These fads are created and promoted because the industry knows they are guaranteed to raise cash. One would think the financial institutions were colluding as virtually every fund family concurrently produces similar products in response to whatever sector is performing best at the time.

> *"The market can remain irrational longer than you can remain solvent."*
> John Maynard Keynes

Here a Bubble, There a Bubble

Remember the commodity bubble that followed the real estate bubble? After oil prices rose from $30 to well over $100 per barrel during the 2000's, a major financial firm's analyst predicted oil would soar to $200 a barrel. The $200 benchmark didn't happen, of course, but a lot of investors lost their shirts following that recommendation. Why didn't their advisors remind them of what happened with real estate and tech stocks? Were they afraid they would lose clients by going against the herd?

Currently, a lot of advisors are chasing performance by moving their clients into big growth tech stocks known as FANG — Facebook, Amazon, Netflix, and Google (Alphabet) — that have done well recently. How long will the FANG bubble last?

Though I am NOT a market timer, there have been a couple of times over the past two decades when it was relatively easy to recognize a bubble forming as valuations became unrealistically high. The commodities bubble was one of those occurrences and I sold our positions during the summer of 2008. I got out of real estate prematurely in 2005 as prices rose even higher before crashing back to earth in 2007. Manias and unrealistic valuations can continue unabated for years. Investors mistakenly believe "this time is different" and chase the newest "sure thing," which continues to soar higher as more investors join the parade. When such rampant speculation occurs, I am happy to surrender some of the potential upside in exchange for keeping our clients away from the devastation ahead. That said, recessions and stock market corrections often occur with no apparent warning. Investors must be willing to simply wait out the storm as the clouds will often break when least expected, as they did during early 2009 when the market finally began its recovery from the worst economic crisis since the Great Depression, beginning what is now one of the longest stock market rallies in history.

Currently, the big rave is alternatives, which encompasses a dizzying array of hedge fund and mutual fund strategies including market neutral, long/short, managed futures, options, derivatives contracts, and private equity to name a few. Mutual fund companies are laboring overtime to pump them out. One mutual fund company's pitch reads: "Goodbye 60/40. Hello 50/30/20," encouraging advisors and investors to invest larger portions of their assets in alternatives.

When advisors ask us to give them an alternative or hedged strategy for their clients, I remind them that the best hedge is the income provided by a balanced portfolio. They say they need a hedging strategy to keep their clients invested when the things go south but frankly, I believe that's a lack of leadership on their part.

Disappointing Performance

The mutual fund industry is all too happy to accommodate their timidity by issuing an endless variety of alternative funds. Advisors are discovering that these funds aren't performing very well, however.

According to a 2018 *Morningstar* article, "It remains to be seen whether alternatives will earn investor loyalty or if the category will be another in a long string of black eyes for the financial services industry. The potential to better investor outcomes seems to be there. Indeed, the interest expressed in the category by credible players such as Vanguard and PIMCO plus the credibility of new players such as AQR and Research Affiliates bodes well for the possibilities of the category. To date, however, the alternatives market still looks too much like the flawed mutual fund marketplace of the 1980s, a time when funds were sold and not bought, than it resembles today's modern, investor-centric fund world. Time will tell if alternatives can break out of this time warp and make a credible contribution to investors' success and the industry's future."[11]

Advisors are now discovering that these alternative funds aren't performing as hoped. Instead of trying to protect their clients using sexy alternative strategies or options, I would argue that they would be better off employing a plain vanilla, 60/40 stock/bond mix that generates a more consistent income stream of dividends and interest. Better to adhere to a simpler, easier to understand approach than constantly running with the herd, chasing the latest option or hedged equity strategy.

I'm constantly amazed that advisors and even institutional investors continue to throw money at hedge funds. At a recent conference, I heard about a hedge fund manager who ran his fund into the ground, closing after losing approximately 70% of the original assets. Two years later, he reemerged with a new fund and immediately attracted a host of institutional investors, eager to give him another chance to manage their money. It's not an isolated incident. The people who run hedge funds are typically very smart and great salesmen. A year or two after imploding, they reappear with a new idea and the consultants and institutions mindlessly donate all over again. Meanwhile, the hedge fund managers get rich despite delivering poor performance and making some horrendous mistakes.

Fund Flows Tell the Story

Herd advisors are as susceptible as individual investors to the influence of Wall Street marketers. Proof can be found in the Morningstar asset flows, reporting billions flowing into alternatives in recent years. That's partially due to individual investors but primarily due to financial advisors and institutions who should know better.

In addition, billions upon billions are flowing into passive strategies. The massive rise of investing in passive index funds — laden with overvalued growth stocks unlike the reasonably priced, dividend stocks we own — is a major contributor to the overvaluations of such large, momentum stocks. Advisors are, once again, acting senselessly, simply investing in passive exchange traded funds (ETFs). Utilized in computer driven algorithms, ETFs react violently and often have to be unwound during tumultuous markets. It's one reason why I'm not a fan of ETFs and even more opposed to exchange traded notes (ETNs) as they are effectively derivatives — or as Warren Buffett calls them, "financial weapons of mass destruction."

While financial marketers love alternatives and hedge funds because they are more profitable, their diminished performance over time as compared to a simple 60/40 stock/bond mix is taking a toll on their popularity.

According to a *Financial Times* piece, "the huge scale of new cash inflows into alternatives in recent years has also driven up valuations across these illiquid assets and raised concerns that investors may be disappointed by future returns that are widely expected to be lower than those achieved historically."[12]

Endowments which adopted the *Yale Model* have underperformed terribly in recent years. The Yale Model suggests that large investors, such as endowments and public pension funds, can achieve superior returns by shifting a significant portion of investments away from traditional stocks and bonds and into carefully selected hedge funds, private equity, real estate, and other alternatives.

Because of the continued lackluster performance, many institutions, including the state of California, will no longer retain hedge fund managers and are moving even more assets into passive strategies.

There is an inherent danger in this massive flow of funds into alternatives and passive strategies. As increasing numbers of investors move into passive ETFs, the largest market cap companies become even larger. It certainly could be the latest bubble and it's a dangerous one because it once again reflects the tendency of advisors and investors to follow the herd over the cliff.

Famous Last Words: We'll Protect You

Herding advisors make it even easier for wholesalers to peddle products mimicking whatever is hot. Insurance and annuity products have particular appeal, enabling advisors to tell their clients: "We're going to protect you on the downside so you don't get hurt by market corrections." It's an easy story to sell, as opposed to telling clients the truth, as I do, which is that if you are in the market, there is no real protection when the next 20% market correction happens and you must be prepared to weather such inevitable volatility as a long-term investor. When clients ask what they can do, I advise that people all over the world are likely to continue drinking Pepsi so hold on to your Pepsi shares and keep collecting the dividend. Don't worry about things outside of your control. We've been through all kinds of strife over the past two decades: Gulf wars, 9/11, the real estate meltdown, yet the world continues to revolve and good companies continue to thrive. Investors who have stayed the course over the past forty years during recessions and market corrections — even during more severe bear market corrections — have recovered in five years or less.

That's not a popular opinion and not what many investors (or media outlets) want to hear. What they want to hear — and what herd advisors tell them — is: "We'll protect you by getting you out of the market when the correction comes, either by liquidating your equities, hedging your portfolio, or putting in stop losses." None of these strategies actually protect investors and, in fact, tend to deteriorate returns over time. Instead, investors should think of investing as owning a company, not merely buying a stock certificate.

I hope to continue helping my clients for many decades to come. How silly would it be for me to wake up one morning and decide to sell my company because I have a headache? Then, after lunch, since I "feel" better, decide to buy it back. And finally, at day's end, feeling tired and worn out, decide to sell it again. It makes no sense but that's what herd advisors and traders on television advise their clients to do with their stocks.

In contrast, I believe it more prudent to passionately and competently pursue long-term investments for our clients. I prefer to think of our investments as buying a piece of a business. We're buying a piece of Proctor & Gamble and we're going to hold that business for the long term unless the valuation becomes untenable. It's trust in a long-term perspective, as opposed to a trading perspective. We're going to collect our income and stay invested. Despite all the turmoil of the past twenty years, none of our retiree clients had to go back to work. None of our clients had to go find jobs during the financial crisis. They just kept collecting their income while patiently waiting for the stock price to recover.

A lot of people who invested in sexy growth stocks that plummeted couldn't collect income and were unable to fund their retirements. They had to alter their retirement outlook and lifestyle. It may have been easier for their advisors to sell them on what was hot and on what would ostensibly protect them against downturns, but it's certainly no easier now for their clients with depleted assets.

The primary reason our clients never had to go back to work is the 4% – 5% income stream produced by their "simple" balanced 60/40 stock/bond portfolio. In contrast, the current environment of passive/alternative/ETFs strategies utilized by the majority of advisors produces little income and incurs only the hope for price appreciation to fund existing or future retirements.

"It's far better to buy a wonderful company at a fair price than a fair company at a wonderful price."
Warren Buffett

CHAPTER FOUR

Advisors and the Fund Complex

Don't Run With the Herd — Go It Alone

Like bell bottoms and pet rocks, investment fads emerge and disappear, leaving behind nothing but historical footnotes.

Producers of financial products have a seemingly infinite capacity for creating seductive investments that ultimately evaporate into the ether. In recent decades, funds embracing the latest craze, from dot.com stocks to real estate to commodities, have all burst upon the scene with great fanfare, sucked untold investors in with their promise of unconstrained growth, then flamed out, leaving the last buyers disillusioned and wondering what happened.

Sadly, unlike those who bought water beds or beanie babies and who learned their lesson after losing a relative pittance, investors who have their portfolios eviscerated by the latest fad never seem to learn. As soon as the next investment mania pulls into the station, they can't wait to buy a ticket and climb aboard the crazy train. The whole revolving circus is a testament to greed, financial marketing genius, and envy as investors fear missing out on the latest fad in which their neighbors are fully participating.

With interest rates at exceptionally low levels, the newest reach for return includes alternative and even "liquid alternative" investments, which have mushroomed since the 2007 financial crisis, as investors and advisors search for a means to dampen volatility and protect the downside risk in their portfolios. This latest fad is exemplified in Warren Buffett's epic $1 million bet with New York money manager Protégé Partners. Buffett wagered that a simple S&P 500 index fund would outperform Protégé's carefully chosen portfolio of hedge funds over 10 years, assuming fees and expenses were included. The contest unofficially ended after 9 years when, lagging the S&P 500 by over 40%, Protégé's co-founder threw in the towel. Protégé was slaughtered because they believed the hedge funds' alternative strategies would pay off and, of course, were dead wrong.

Loosely defined, alternative investments can include anything that isn't effectively a publicly traded stock or bond. This includes less liquid hedge funds and potentially more liquid mutual funds investing in assets and strategies as widely varied as fine wine, art, private equity, derivatives, commodities, managed futures, long-short, market neutral and real estate, to name just a few. According to Morningstar, there were just 269 mutual funds and ETFs categorized in the alternative global broad category group at the beginning of 2007, whereas today there are over 1,500 funds that could be classified as liquid alternatives. Clearly, fund companies are ramping up production as advisors take the bait. In a July 2015 survey by Barron's and Morningstar, 63% of financial advisors stated they planned to allocate more than 11% of their clients' portfolios to alternatives in the next five years – up from 39% of advisors a year earlier.[13]

Despite empirical evidence to the contrary, institutional investors are also not immune to the siren call of alternative strategies. In the past week, our firm received two requests for proposals, one from the human resources department of a large state and another from a sovereign government in Asia.

The HR asked for proposals on a global tactical allocation for their $14 billion defined contribution plan. It stipulated that they would only consider proposals for strategies that are designed to provide a real rate of return of the CPI plus 4% and that the strategy should invest tactically in globally diversified asset classes that provide a low correlation to stocks and bonds.

Ostensibly, this is what the highly educated people running institutional portfolios consider prudent investing. If my firm was to reply that we were going to allocate to a traditional mix of stocks and bonds, they would simply toss our proposal out. They would prefer to hear proposals from firms that have "jazzed up" option strategies, utilize leverage and employ non-correlated gunk to dampen volatility. These brilliant MBAs and CFAs have bought into the hype of alternatives and the promise of higher returns with lower risk which, of course, is not feasible.

Some institutional investors have recently regained their sanity and decided (finally) that they can no longer justify hedge fund fees as they weren't adding value. Thus, they are now shifting gears and hiring separate account managers. The rub, however, is that they are essentially asking asset managers like us — whose fees are lower — to essentially do the same hazardous, ineffective things the hedge funds were doing. They eschew traditional balanced funds or strategies that adhere to a static allocation approach, clearly remaining entrenched in the latest fad of alternatives. Of note, the Harvard University endowment fund recently fired their manager because of poor performance — driven primarily by the fund's alternative strategies. This is the problem with alternatives; they simply don't work well over extended periods.

Option strategies are also gaining great popularity among retail investors. Custodians such as Schwab, E*trade, and Fidelity continuously run ads touting their benefit and the ease of usage without mentioning how it drives up the investor's cost (thereby reducing return) while pumping up the custodian's profitability. A prospective client approached one of our advisors, desiring to get involved with option strategies to increase his income. The request sounds reasonable on its face and in theory can work; however, it often doesn't pan out in a positive manner when put into practice.

Consider the case of a stock paying a 4% dividend. Suppose that an investor decides he isn't satisfied with the dividend and growth potential and wishes to squeeze some extra income out of it by writing a covered call.[14] However, stock prices often move in fits and spurts, deriving a portion of their return in a rapid move higher. Under such a scenario, a stock which moves 10% or 15% during a month would be called away, thereby negating much of the total return potential of the company since a covered call option "caps" your upside return during a short period of time. While some investors rationalize using options to hedge against a stock's decline, doing so deteriorates the return of the stock over time because of the hedging cost. Here again, the investor is thinking like a trader rather than an investor in a company for the long term.

Investors also often fret about a stock's price decline and desire to place stop losses on their positions. However, if you like a company at $20, why wouldn't you like it just as much at $15 after a 25% decline? I'm in the only business wherein people spurn a 25% discount and sell an asset they loved just last week!

Bitcoin — a Major Mania

As Bitcoin skyrocketed higher, and the media began reporting regularly about the phenomenon, one of my uncles asked me what I thought about it. I did my best to explain that valuing Bitcoin wasn't something that could be accomplished. I advised him that it wasn't like his electrical company since it doesn't generate profits. I told him that based on the profit his company generates, we could place a value on it that makes sense. I also told him that I didn't believe that Bitcoin was even a currency, asking him if I could pay him in Bitcoin after he installed a few new lights in my house.

Bitcoin cannot be classified as a currency since a nation's currency (U.S. dollar, Japanese yen, Swiss franc, etc.) must act as a sound store of value and medium of exchange—with the exception of unstable nations. Certainly, something which may fluctuate 25% in a few hours cannot be a store of value nor be utilized to exchange it for a service or good (such as hamburger) as the vendor receiving payment in Bitcoin cannot rely on its certainty.

While the distributed ledger technology (blockchain) may disrupt industries like title companies and custodians, it's uncertain as to whether Bitcoin and other cryptocurrencies will grow into accepted currencies and a medium of exchange. We are unlikely to know the answer until the next global crisis. A currency is only as stable as the entity (generally a sovereign nation) producing it, and is commonly supported and influenced by that country's trade balance, GDP, debt, monetary policy and inflation, among other economic indicators. My assumption is that Bitcoin is not sustained by any of the aforementioned economic factors and is merely supported by investor sentiment.

Even well-established currencies are notoriously difficult to assess or trade. Will individuals be comfortable holding onto Bitcoin during the next recession? How will they react during a financial crisis like the last one when they question who is backing the cryptocurrency? Some might argue that Bitcoin has more value than traditional currencies since there is a fixed amount and it cannot be created. But is that true? Why can't more be created?

As Bitcoin's upward surge approached 20,000 in late 2017, financial news couldn't stop talking about the phenomenon. Investors scampered to get a piece of the action, fearing they would miss out on the next big thing. In the span of a week, Bitcoin was down 25%. During the first month of 2018, its market value was reduced by more than half from its high. The fear of missing out drives many money managers and their advisors right into the bonfire, where they are often quickly incinerated.

For me, there are certain economic principles that are written in blood. Overpaying for an asset based upon unrealistic growth potential is certainly one principle in finance which should never be ignored. Whether it's tulip mania, the dot.com bubble, or Bitcoin, the enticement to get in before you lose out can be irresistible. As Warren Buffett so wisely said, "You don't have to swing at every pitch." Buffett, one of the world's acknowledged masters of investing, certainly missed out on early opportunities to invest in both Amazon and Google. However, despite those oversights, he's done pretty darn well. One of the wonderful things about investing is that you don't have to be right 100% of the time. You can stick to your principles and not chase manias which can quickly lead to the destruction of your portfolio.

Even really smart people are seduced by fads, believing they can make money because eager new investors continue to arrive every day. They ignore historical precedence and convince themselves that it's going to keep going up and up. How often have I heard them say, "This time it's different!"

It's important to read and understand economic history. I was very young during the 1973-75 energy crisis and recession, but well remember the gas lines and the high inflation of the seventies. Black Monday in 1987, the recessions in the early 1990's and 2000's, including the dot-com bubble, September 11th attacks, and the Great Recession caused by the subprime mortgage crisis and housing bubble, all had indelible marks on my life and financial career. I wasn't around however during the Panic of 1873 and subsequent Long Depression, Panic of 1907, or the Great Depression, but continue to study and learn important economic and financial lessons from these and other historical events. As Mark Twain is reputed to have said: "History doesn't repeat itself, but it often rhymes." Lessons learned from previous fads and bubbles — such as early century technological (radio, automobiles, aviation) or more recent advancements in high tech, internet, and healthcare — should serve as reminders that valuation always matters.

Today's Wall Street offices are crammed with newly minted MBAs and CFAs—many of whom were born in the early nineties—conjuring up investment ideas. They don't remember the 2000 tech stock bubble or the crash of 1987. If they remember the real estate bubble or ensuing financial crisis, it's only vaguely since many were still young teenagers. As Wall Street rewards youthful optimism and new ideas that generate fresh profits, the lessons of these economic events are little studied or remembered. These new executives are too busy building mathematical algorithms and conjuring up the next sexy product which they can push on a receptive audience believing in new magical formulas.

CHAPTER FIVE

Fads, Manias and Alternatives

Listen Attentively Before You Leave the Burrow

On a visit to Six Flags Great Adventure in New Jersey, my oldest daughter, just 6 or 7 at the time, insisted we ride El Toro, the famous wooden rollercoaster. As we climbed the first hill and the coaster's wheels clicked away, she was suddenly seized with fear and began screaming "I want to get off!" I took her hand and reassured her as best I could. When the ride was over, she screamed again, this time with glee at having overcome her fear.

If it had been possible for her to jump out as the coaster climbed and clanked, she would have likely perished. Instead, having remained on the ride during that first thrilling plunge and the succeeding twists and turns, she survived and was better and more confident for the experience.

Investing can be like that rollercoaster ride. At times, it can be frightening and make you wish you had never gotten on, but by staying in your seat and trusting that the coaster has solid construction and will stay on the track, you ultimately are rewarded with a fulfilling, if sometimes daunting, experience.

I often relate that story to clients when they are tempted to abandon ship during times of market turbulence. Like a cross country flight, you can't jump out of the plane at the first sign of turbulence. You must simply tighten your seat belt and ride it out with the confidence that you will safely arrive at your destination as the odds are much greater with you than if you panic and take rash actions.

Warren Buffett believes trying to time the market and trying to mimic high-frequency traders are two of investors' biggest mistakes. He notes, "People that think they can predict the short-term movement of the stock market — or listen to other people who talk about timing the market — are making a big mistake. So is trying to mimic high-frequency traders. Buying stock in a good business and hanging on for the long term is a better strategy than flipping stocks like a short-order cook flips pancakes. If they are trading actively, they are making a big mistake."[15]

I wholeheartedly agree with the "Sage of Omaha." Market timing only works if you are omniscient. When investing, I believe technical analysis and market timing are about as useful as astrology. But because gullible investors continue their search for a magic formula, market timing schemes continue to flourish.

The fact that hundreds of investment funds plying timing strategies fail every year doesn't dissuade investors from chasing the latest iteration. It's not just individual investors who fall prey to thinking there is a way to predict market movements: highly compensated institutional investors and investment managers display the same speculative senselessness. Given that those who are purportedly the "best and brightest" on Wall Street fail at such an alarming rate, what chance does the average investor have of outguessing the market?

Consider the massive amount of money and resources major brokerage firms throw at technical analysis in an effort to prognosticate whether the market will zig or zag tomorrow. If all that effort and expense still results in hundreds of investment funds failing every year, what makes someone with an idea and an iPad think he has a better chance of success?

There is ample statistical validation for remaining fully invested. The following chart depicts the startling impact of missing out on just a few of the best days over a period of 20 years.

I don't believe anyone can consistently and accurately time short-term swings in markets or inflection points in market cycles. The false belief that they can be timed often leads to performance-chasing, whipsawing in and out of markets (selling low and buying high), and ultimately disappointing investment results. What's more, it is often when "the experts" are overwhelmingly aligned on one side of a trade and the consensus is strongest that a trend will continue, that it actually has the greatest potential to reverse.

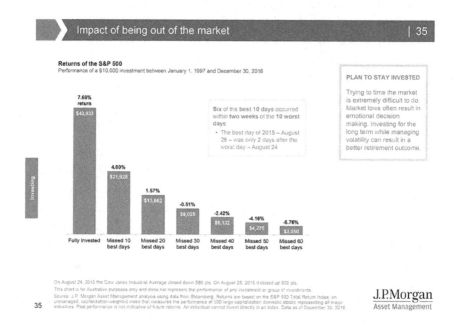

Fig. 5.1: Impact of being out of the market

Market timing schemes may sound plausible, even logical, but they rarely work in practice—especially over time. That's why I have always focused on attempting to achieve the market's return with less risk and volatility while providing better income through dividends.

This is not an easily maintained conviction as Wall Street and a compliant media tantalize investors with captivating tales of stock market success based on speculative strategies. You no doubt have seen the ubiquitous commercials about the retired airline pilot who developed an online trading strategy that wondrously turned an investment of $40,000 into an account that generates $50,000 in annual income. Evidently driven by altruistic instincts, he is now willing to share his magical formula with the world via his book, available for only the cost of shipping and handling, of course. Question: If his system actually worked, why would he bother to write a book giving away his secrets, and then spend money to advertise it?

"Without doubt, the most serious mistake individual investors make is trying to time the market. I have never known anyone who knows anyone who has consistently made accurate directional bets on either equity or bond prices."

Burton G Malkiel,
A Random Walk Down Wall Street

Much of what marketers peddle to ostensibly beat the system is based on appealing to investors' basic instincts. If I were able to set aside honor and ethics, I could easily become a financial snake oil salesman. It's all too easy to prey upon investors' fear and greed to make a fortune. The same holds true for those who hawk market timing services as I (like Warren Buffett) believe it is an impossibility to time if/when corrections will occur over any period of time. This is especially true as one has to get the timing correct at both the bottom and the top.

When individual investors try to time the market, they are much more likely to buy and sell at the worst times. Emotionally, investors suffer great pain when pessimism is rampant and stock prices fall. They are more likely to buy when everyone is optimistic and prices are near or at their peak. Behavioral considerations cause investors all too often to shoot themselves in the foot.[16]

Time in the market, not timing the market, is what matters most. What market timers often fail to understand is that missing out on even a small number of good days can eviscerate long-term portfolio returns. The more moves in and out of the market made, the greater the chances for missing some of the best market days.

Market timing is inalterably tied to financial, economic or political events that propel the decision to get in or out of the market. But why would you make investment decisions with long-term ramifications based on transitory events?

"Don't try to buy at the bottom and sell at the top. It can't be done except by liars."

Bernard Baruch

Maintaining a degree of equanimity is a valuable attribute of successful long-term investors. Global risks always exist and unexpected events inevitably happen, causing markets to fall no matter their valuation. The world and financial markets have faced numerous negative shocks over the decades, but the broad economic impacts have ultimately proved transitory. Over the long term, financial assets are priced and valued based on their underlying economic fundamentals — yields, earnings, growth — not on transitory macro events or who occupies the White House.

Investors benefit by not reacting to every domestic political development or geopolitical event with the urge to sell their stocks, nor get overly excited and jump into the market on some piece of news they view positively. I don't believe refraining from such short-term trades is complacency — if the choice is supported by a sound decision-making framework. A disciplined investment process and a focus on the long term are essential to best achieve your financial objectives.

Great American companies will continue to grow regardless of idiotic politicians, even should our nation move toward a European socialism. Terrific international companies such as Nestle, Royal Dutch Shell, and Diageo have performed exceptionally well under socialism as capitalism always finds an outlet somewhere in the world where these companies flourish. What impact does the election of any candidate — or any other exogenous event — have on how many McDonald's hamburgers are consumed in China, Nestle chocolate or Intel chips in Latin America or Pepsi Cola in Africa or India? Virtually none.

> *"In the long run it doesn't matter much whether your timing is great or lousy. What matters is that you stay invested."*
> Louis Rukeyser, Wall Street Week

I don't know if the current stock rally will persist unabated or if high yield bond prices will rise or fall in the coming year. I am not concerned with short term movements. Just as I don't look at the daily price of my business, I don't worry about the prices of stocks and high yield bonds on a daily, monthly, quarterly or even annual basis. I understand that while prices will fluctuate, income from the dividends and interest generated by our portfolio tends to remain relatively stable. This provides our clients with the income necessary to potentially fund retirement needs or be reinvested to purchase additional shares.

As an investor, I don't have to be right 100% of the time in order to attain a sound rate of return. I am naturally concerned when losses occur but price declines are a natural and healthy aspect of investing. Fools who chase momentum on the up or down side get hammered as they whipsaw from position to position. There will always be defaults and investments that don't perform well. While mistakes are unavoidable, risk can be managed by avoiding leverage, not investing a large amount in any one position, and not running at the first sight of trouble, instead remaining invested for the long run.

"Do nothing. I think all of this market timing is statistically unfounded. I don't trust it. You may avoid a downturn, but you may also miss the rise. Choose the risk tolerance you're OK with and hold tight."
Professor Eugene Fama

CHAPTER SIX

Leverage and Options Strategies

Don't Borrow Money from the Elephants,
Run with the Gazelles or Gamble with the Monkeys

Leverage is the investment strategy of using *borrowed money*, specifically, the use of various financial instruments or borrowed capital to increase the potential return of an investment. The borrowed money can come from a variety of sources, the most common of which are brokerage margin loans, futures contracts, and options or similar derivative securities.

Both margin loans and futures contracts leave investors exposed to considerable downside risk. Declines in the underlying security can lead to large percentage losses and may require the investor to immediately provide additional funds or risk being sold out of their position at a loss.[17]

From an investor's perspective, leverage can be gained by using a margin account. If you open a million-dollar account with a major brokerage firm or online discount firm, they will generally allow you to borrow 50% — or a half million — on margin. Or, if you want to borrow a few hundred thousand against your portfolio to buy that 60-ft yacht you've always wanted, your broker will be happy to lend you the money. After all, the firm now not only makes money on the commissions from trades, but also makes interest on your loan — a win-win for the broker. The danger in this action occurs if (really when as market corrections are normal) the market suffers a significant correction. You will then suffer the fate of a margin call, which could mean having to liquidate securities that have been beaten down. It's one reason why I always recommend avoiding the use of leverage.

The seminal example of the hazards of leverage is Long-Term Capital Portfolio L.P., a hedge fund that used absolute-return trading strategies combined with high financial leverage[18]. Long Term Capital Management (LTCM) was founded in 1994 by John W. Meriwether, the former vice-chairman and head of bond trading at Salomon Brothers. Members of LTCM's board of directors included Myron S. Scholes and Robert C. Merton, who shared the 1997 Nobel Memorial Prize in Economic Sciences for a "new method to determine the value of derivatives." Initially successful with an annualized return of over 21% (after fees) in its first year, 43% in the second year and 41% in the third year, in 1998 it lost $4.6 billion in less than four months following the 1997 Asian financial crisis and 1998 Russian financial crisis, requiring financial intervention by the Federal Reserve, with the fund liquidating and dissolving in early 2000.[19]

This historic collapse was overseen by some of the smartest financial minds on the planet, people with PhDs in Economics that won a Nobel Prize. Their collective genius managed to create a hedge fund that accumulated so much systemic risk, it took a $3 billion bailout from sixteen of the world's largest banks to restore investor confidence in the markets.

As Warren Buffett remarked in his 2010 shareholder letter, "When leverage works, it magnifies your gains. Your spouse thinks you're clever, and your neighbors get envious. But leverage is addictive. Once having profited from its wonders, very few people retreat to more conservative practices. And as we all learned in third grade — and some relearned in 2008 — any series of positive numbers, however impressive the numbers may be, evaporates when multiplied by a single zero. History tells us that leverage all too often produces zeroes, even when it is employed by very smart people."[20]

Options

Options are a type of derivative security in which the option's price is linked to the price of something else. Alternative investments that use options to ostensibly enhance returns can be alluring, right up to the point where the strategy collapses. How would you like to have been one of the investors (hopefully you weren't) in the LJM Preservation and Growth Fund who received an email one morning stating that the strategy had suffered "significant losses?" That was quite an understatement as the fund plunged over 80% during the first week of February, 2018.

The email, signed by LJM's Founder and Chairman Tony Caine, said (incredibly) that the firm's goal was to "preserve as much capital as possible by hedging with as many futures as possible to attempt to insulate portfolios from further losses." He caveated that their "ability to do so depends on market conditions and liquidity."

Evidently, the "preservation" aspect of the fund's options strategy failed to take into consideration what was deemed to be the insignificant factor of market conditions and liquidity.

A large Registered Investment Advisory firm I know well replaced its long-only bond positions with an alternative strategy in an attempt to reach for yield for its clients. In doing so, the firm, with its pedigreed Ivy League educated investment committee, constructed a fund of funds with complex alternative strategies which included the LJM Preservation and Growth Fund. I cautioned the firm's principal about the dangers of a portfolio in which the risks couldn't be measured and suggested an approach I preferred: simply owning individual bonds in companies I could understand. He scoffed at such an approach and displayed his enigmatic, back-tested formulas that predicted his portfolio would produce higher returns than ours with less risk. The story's ending — how our firm's "boring" strategy subsequently provided a sounder approach for our clients — needs no further explanation.

So many of these alternative strategies employing options or leverage produce, at best, mediocre returns and, at worst, fail miserably, leaving carnage in their wake.

Leveraged Failures

The basic concept of financial leverage is taking the proceeds of a loan and investing that money to receive a higher rate of return. The difference in the rates (the interest rate of the loan and interest rate earned on the investment) is called the spread.

Investment banks, hedge funds, money managers, and investors often borrow money from others through deposits or loans and pay a fixed interest rate on the debt. Then they take that borrowed money and invest it, expecting, of course, to achieve a higher return. At a traditional bank, deposits — such as savings accounts or CDs — earn a low interest rate and the money is then loaned out at higher interest rates to businesses for investment in capital projects or to individuals to purchase homes.

The U.S. Banking Act of 1933 separated commercial and investment banking. Beginning in the early 1960's, this law was gradually deregulated, culminating in its complete gutting in 1999 with the Gramm-Leach-Bliley Act. Signing the Act, President Bill Clinton publicly declared it "will enhance the stability of our financial services system." Under the Act, large financial institutions such as insurance companies, commercial banks, and investment banks are able to operate under the same corporate umbrella.

As one of a small minority in the financial services industry, I believe in separating these institutions by bringing back Glass Steagall provisions to help mitigate the risk of another financial crisis requiring a large government bailout. In the post- Great Recession, spurred by the subprime mortgage crisis of 2007-2009, large banks have only grown larger. Of course, these large banks, many of which we invest in, vociferously defend deregulation. Though the next financial crisis may be decades away, corporations, by nature, will attempt to maximize profits and eventually take on too much leverage and risk leading to their demise. No bank can survive a run when everyone heads for the exits, and only the federal government can backstop such an economic calamity.

On a simpler, microeconomic scale, imagine that Altrius Capital is a hedge fund (a highly unlikely scenario due to my ethical reservations) managing $350 million. Under the Altrius entity, assume that we also owned a commercial bank, Altrius Trust, which has $350 million in deposits from local business owners and individuals. Now assume that the Altrius hedge fund arm takes a dangerous gamble (like the other hedge fund manager mistakes previously mentioned) by borrowing $175 million and investing all $525 million in a risky growth stock or a short bet that coffee would decline in price. When the price of this trade implodes, leading to massive losses, the commercial bank Altrius Trust would be taken down with the hedge fund — particularly as news hits the street and depositors demand their bank holdings back immediately...which, of course, have also been lent out to other businesses and individuals. Should this occur, the entire company would be taken down and depositors would need to be bailed out by the government through FDIC insurance.

Lehman Brothers was the fourth biggest investment bank in America until it filed for the bankruptcy in September 2008, less than a year after the bank presented its biggest profit ever.

Like all of the large banks, Lehman Brothers borrowed money in order to invest in mortgage-backed securities (MBS) as well as a variety of other investments. In the case of the MBS, when the real estate assets used as collateral for those mortgage-backed securities fell precipitously in price, the MBS became worth a great deal less, driving Lehman Brothers' spread from positive to negative. All of the major banks were leveraged at high ratios but Lehman's was even more so with $639 billion in assets and $619 billion in debt.[21]

The effect of the high leverage ratio reduced investors' confidence, creating a negative feedback loop making the downfall fast and unstoppable. It's one reason why the 158-year old bank could collapse just one year after its most profitable year ever. Unlike Bear Stearns' fire sale to JP Morgan early that year in which the Federal Reserve provided a backstop for its MBS, the Fed this time foolishly backed away from such provisions, driving away any potential buyers. The result was not only the collapse of Lehman Brothers and the loss of employment for its 25,000 employees worldwide, but also a full-blown panic for the entire financial system.

At the time, Fed chairman Ben Bernanke, Treasury Secretary Henry Paulson, and New York Fed President Tim Geithner argued that they did not have the authority to rescue Lehman Brothers due to the size of its debts. Amazingly, just days later, the officials somehow found the authority to provide AIG with a $180 billion bailout — necessary as AIG sold credit default swaps which insured the assets supporting corporate debt and mortgages. If AIG had gone bankrupt, it would have triggered the bankruptcy of many of the large financial institutions that purchased these swaps as insurance.

The bailout of AIG came one day after Treasury Secretary Paulson said there would be no further Wall Street bailouts. Later that week, Paulson and Bernanke went to Congress requesting a $700 billion bailout to rescue all of the banks. Many on both sides of Congress resisted bailout plans; after initially voting it down, however, the market plummeted, forcing even the recalcitrant in Congress to realize the error of their ways and that they needed to act. Though many lessons may be learned from the crisis and the errors committed by many actors, the enduring moral is that we remain exposed to the risk of the financial system's demise and that leverage is the main ingredient in this horrid soup.

Leverage was at the center of many of the mistakes made during the financial crisis. Individuals displayed little financial responsibility by purchasing homes they couldn't afford. Pressured to keep up with revenue goals, commercial banks lent 100% of home values, even though real estate prices were exceptionally high and many individuals had questionable credit. Investment banks took those loans, packaged them into complex collateralized debt obligations (CDOs), and sold them to anyone (primarily institutional investors like mutual funds, hedge funds, insurance companies, pension funds, and sovereign nations) who would purchase them. Hedge funds and investment banks also purchased CDOs for their asset management portfolio and utilized leverage since "real estate would never decrease in value." Ratings agencies, such as Moody's, Standard and Poor's, and Fitch, sprinkled their imprimatur on the CDOs, giving them AAA ratings. Not to be absolved, Congress deregulated much of the oversight of the financial system and passed laws which encouraged home ownership and a favorable capital gains tax which encouraged flipping homes.

After the financial crisis, you would think investors would react to the next leveraged gambit with painstaking caution. How is it they can so quickly forget how CDOs and leverage decimated the banking industry and sent the financial markets into a plummeting tailspin? An awful lot of investors, including institutional investors, should have known better.

The dangers of leveraged ETFs have been highlighted in the media but investors are slow to learn. Hundreds of leveraged ETFs have failed during the past two years and many are now restructuring. It's an experiment that failed.

Brad Bennett, FINRA Executive Vice President and Chief of Enforcement, explained, "The complexity of leveraged and inverse exchange-traded products makes it essential for securities firms and their representatives to understand these products before recommending them to their customers. Firms must also conduct reasonable due diligence on these and other complex products, sufficiently train their sales force and have adequate supervisory systems in place before offering them to retail investors."

Leveraged funds come and go or are merged. Many open to great fanfare, only to fail in the first year or two due to poor performance or being unsustainable due to insufficient asset growth. After they collapse, many of these fund managers reappear, having folded into an existing fund or running a fund with a new (and exciting) moniker, employing the latest "can't miss" strategy.

It's amazing that institutional investors, responsible for prudently managing their clients' assets, are willing to blindly charge down the same debris-strewn path that led them to disaster in the recent past. The requirement for this position must be similar to that of a baseball relief pitcher: you must have a short memory.

Hedge funds have a history of chasing the latest performance fad and suffering consequences. A 2006 published paper titled, "Why Do Hedge Funds Stop Reporting Their Performance?" investigated two competing hypotheses regarding the reasons for cessation of reporting by hedge funds to data-gathering services. Some authors argue that poor performance, and indeed failure, is the main reason for the cessation of reporting, while others have suggested that funds stop reporting because they do not need to attract new capital; that is, success, and not failure, explains the cessation of reporting. The empirical evidence in this study refutes the latter hypothesis. All three findings suggest the same conclusion: most funds stop reporting not because they are "too successful," but rather due to poor performance.

The fact that hedge funds cease reporting because of unfavorable results implies that failure rates are extremely high. While some hedge funds have provided generous returns, investors face a high risk of buying a poorly performing fund or, even worse, a failing one. Moreover, since failure rates remain high, even for longstanding funds, this risk cannot be mitigated by restricting one's purchases to funds with a long record of past success.[22]

Another hedge fund plunge was reported by Bloomberg LP in an article detailing the losses of John Paulson's Merger Arbitrage Fund: "Paulson is now re-focusing his firm on his founding strategy — merger arbitrage — despite some disastrous returns in recent years. The Paulson Partners Enhanced fund, which uses *borrowed money* to double down, sunk 23 percent in the first two months of 2018, according to a person familiar with the matter, after plunging about 70 percent over the past four years. The losses come amid a fund revamp at Paulson's namesake firm, once one of the biggest in the industry. It will return money to investors in some funds including the Credit Opportunities, Bloomberg News reported Friday. Investors in that credit fund can transfer their capital to a separate pool or they'll be forced to redeem. It's a sobering turnabout for Paulson, who shot to fame and fortune a decade ago with a dramatic, winning bet against the U.S. housing market. But after a series of missteps, the firm's assets under management have dwindled to about $9 billion from a $38 billion peak in 2011. Most of what's left belongs to Paulson himself."[23]

Over longer periods of time, even the best performing alternative funds have 3 and 5-year track records that have underperformed a simple, old fashioned 60/40 global income strategy. Endowments like Harvard and Yale have similarly learned that the complex alternative strategies they used delivered mediocre results, at best, over extended periods. They would likely have been better off emulating Warren Buffett's bet: buying the S&P 500 and holding it long term.

On Borrowing

One of the mistakes I emphasize that clients avoid is borrowing against their portfolio. It's a harmful and potentially destructive blunder. Had Warren Buffett been leveraged when his stock plunged 50% in the 1973 stock market correction, Berkshire Hathaway would have gone bankrupt. It's unlikely the financial world would have ever heard of "The Sage of Omaha."

When the tide goes out and you're swimming naked, there is simply nowhere to hide. Depending on the amount of leverage you utilize and your portfolio's percentage decline, you may have a margin call. This is a broker's demand that you pay him back, either with cash from outside your portfolio or by selling some or all of your securities in order to meet the broker's minimum maintenance margin. As an investor, you should never use leverage or borrow against your portfolio. Though it may be enticing to attempt to juice your returns in investments you believe are terrific, the unthinkable can and will eventually happen and you will be left naked on the beach wondering what happened.

As an example, let's say I manage a $100 million hedge fund and I put the entire amount my clients and investors have given me into a 10% bond. However, I may not be satisfied with the 10% return, so to try to enhance my return, I borrow $50 million on margin from my brokerage account and buy another $50 million of the same company's bond. I have now invested $150 million in total. What happens if the company goes bankrupt?

Not only do my investors lose everything they gave me, but they owe more money. "How can I owe more than I invested," they ask? Well, I lost $150 million, not just the original $100 million, because I wasn't happy with that 10% return. I wanted a 15% return for my investors so I used leverage and borrowed another $50 million. I didn't borrow to *buy* something, I leveraged the portfolio to try and get a better return. What Warren Buffett has said many times, and what I am in total agreement with, is *never use leverage in your portfolio*. Not only can you lose your investment, you can lose even more money than you invested and possibly face bankruptcy.

Ignore the avalanche of TV commercials touting the money to be made using option strategies and leverage. The big money they refer to is for them, not you. The Wall Street brokers and bank advisors who hype borrowing against your portfolio are doubling down on their fees.

The Financial Industry Regulatory Authority (FINRA) warns against using your portfolio as collateral:

"With stock indices hitting record highs recently, taking out a loan against your portfolio may seem like an easy way to get access to cash without having to sell securities. But if the market slips, investors borrowing against their accounts can quickly find themselves in a bind."

If there's a decline in the value of the securities collateralizing a loan, lenders can demand that borrowers put up more collateral on short notice. If a borrower doesn't pony up the extra collateral within the designated time frame, the lender then has the right to sell as many of the securities as necessary, potentially without the investor's input on which ones to sell and which to hold. This can also result in unexpected and adverse tax consequences for the borrower.

In some instances, a lender could skip straight to selling the assets without first offering a borrower the chance to deposit cash or additional collateral into the account. In either case, the borrower might be left with unexpected tax obligations and other fees.

But borrowers have to be on their guard even if the stock market isn't crashing. Many brokers reserve the right to call back a securities-based loan at any time, for any reason.

Things can really get tricky if a lender comes calling and an investor has already spent his or her borrowed money on something that isn't easy to sell right away, such as a house, or can't be returned, like college tuition payments.

Warren Buffett warns against going into debt to buy stocks, but that's exactly what investors are doing in record numbers. The inevitable, sudden market declines make Buffett skittish about borrowing to buy stocks. In one of his classic annual letters to shareholders, Buffett illustrated the sharp drawdowns Berkshire Hathaway's stock experienced over the years.

Period	High	Low
March 1973 - January 1975	93	38
10/2/1987 - 10/27/1987	4,250	2,675
6/19/1998 - 3/10/2000	80,900	41,300
9/19/2008 - 3/5/2009	147,000	72,400

Fig. 6.1 Stock Movements

"This table offers the strongest argument I can muster against ever using borrowed money to own stocks," Buffett said. "There is simply no telling how far stocks can fall in a short period. Even if your borrowings are small and your positions aren't immediately threatened by the plunging market, your mind may well become rattled by scary headlines and breathless commentary."[24]

When it comes to mistakes, using leverage or margin borrowing against your investment accounts is right near the top in terms of madness.

You might want an addition for your home, perhaps a new master suite that's going to cost $150 thousand. What you should never do is go into your investment account or 401k plan and borrow against it. If your bank is willing to loan you the money at a reasonable rate because you have sufficient equity in the property, okay...maybe. There's risk involved but at least you have a fixed loan and if you have the income to support the higher house payment and adhere to the rule of keeping your housing expense below 25% of your income, that's infinitely better than borrowing against your portfolio. If the bank won't give you the loan, what they're telling you is you probably shouldn't be doing this right now. Even if the bank is willing, you probably should consider whether this is something you need to do or just something you want to do.

As someone trying to prevent investors from making major blunders, insisting a client not do something unwise that may jeopardize his financial well-being can be delicate and often difficult. The disagreement may even lead to a severed relationship, but I would rather protect someone from harming himself and lose him as a client than let him set off a bomb in his own airplane. I have a maxim at Altrius that we will always tell the truth and give our best advice — even should it endanger our relationship. Sometimes, the client is not always right.

CHAPTER SEVEN

Media Madness

Drowning Out the Jungle Mayhem

The financial media is one of the most persuasive — and corrosive — influences on investor behavior. As a resource for credible investment guidance, it's on a par with the guy selling tip sheets at the racetrack. If you choose just one influence to avoid, I suggest you make it the financial news media.

The financial news used to be provided primarily by print media and one or two TV shows like Louis Rukeyser's *Wall Street Week* whose guests included people worth listening to such as legendary investors John Templeton and Peter Lynch. The show, as Rukeyser used to say, "Isn't just about investing; it's about anything that affects people and their money." Guests like Alan Greenspan, Milton Friedman, and Ayn Rand had something of substance to offer viewers and the one-hour conversational format provided the time for them to delineate their long-term perspectives on the markets, economy, and related topics.

In 1980, CNN created the first 24-hour news show. The following year, newcomer CNBC acquired the Financial News Network and the desperate need to fill 24/7 air time with content was born.

The same rule holds true for the financial news as anything else on commercial television: the content is sponsored by advertisers, and if enough people aren't watching, the advertisers take their money elsewhere. The networks can't sell advertising at high rates unless audience measurement models support the cost so financial shows have to maintain a fabricated level of excitement. To keep viewers watching, the shows employ a variety of verbal and visual artifices.

For example, the numerous infusions of "breaking news," which used to signal a consequential event had occurred, but now is simply a device used 20 times a day to regain the attention of viewers who might have nodded off or left the TV to grab a snack.

A column by journalist Mike Skrobin notes that, "In today's world of crisis and scandal it is as important as ever to have a reliable news media to inform the American public about current events and what is going on in this world we all live in. Television news profits have become a higher priority than informing the public, which has created an American population obsessed with celebrity gossip and social networking and naive to worldly events and corrupt politicians. As quoted by Mark Twain, "There are laws to protect the freedom of the press's speech, but none that are worth anything to protect the people from the press." The American people are severely ill informed on a variety of basic government positions and situations, yet overly conscious of the personal lives of talentless celebrities. It is apparent that we as an American public are systematically being dumbed down by our media."[25]

Another ploy is the ubiquitous "you won't believe what we learned about..." plug, inserted to keep viewers tuned in while they are treated to a commercial for some guy named Chuck who ostensibly is an investment genius willing to share his secret formula for beating the market with the unwashed masses for the pittance of postage on his new book.

A clearly effective gimmick is the use of hyperbole when referring to stock movements: "Ford Motor Company is cratering today!" may indicate nothing more than the stock is down a couple percent, but the dramatic inflection is likely to send investors scurrying to their online trading accounts in a futile effort to take action from news of the earth-shattering announcement. Pity the poor investors who are unable to get their brokers on the line or quickly key a few strokes with their discount brokerage firm to liquidate their Ford stock shares! Of course, a couple of hours or days later, the stock has often rebounded and the media invites some money manager or brokerage firm analyst to explain what happened, which they do with great after-the-fact aplomb.

"Anything can happen anytime in markets. And no advisor, economist, or TV commentator – and definitely not Charlie nor I – can tell you when chaos will occur. Market forecasters will fill your ear but will never fill your wallet."
Warren Buffett

There exists an incestuous relationship between the media and the members of the financial industry who buy advertising. Much of the money spent on ads that allows financial news shows to remain on the air is provided by (surprise!) financial custodian firms that promote trading, peddling the preposterous idea that anyone can beat the market if given the "right" information and investment tools. Virtually every E*trade, Schwab, and Fidelity commercial is geared towards trading because that's how they make their money. The more investors trade, the more options they trade, the more money the custodians make. They want viewers engaged, raptly absorbed in option strategies and other trading activity that generates revenue for the sponsors — and keeps Joe Kernen, Stuart Varney, Todd Benjamin, Jim Cramer and an endless list of others on the air, offering their opinions on what will happen in the markets tomorrow, none of which has any tangible impact on what does happen tomorrow.

"Trading can be hazardous to your wealth."
Professor Terrance Odean

It hurts my ears to hear some talking head expound on the reasons why the market is up or down, or (breaking news!) what the market will do tomorrow. It's like listening to the doubletalk of politicians or press secretaries. I suppose the investment managers who guest on financial media expect their appearance will be good for business, even as they are assailed by the host to predict the direction of the market or to "tell us about some stocks you like." It's hard to imagine investors would actually risk their money on such force-fed speculation, but research indicates there is a cause and effect related to these guesswork episodes. There's certainly no shortage of managers and analysts willing to subject themselves to this interrogation, indeed many of them seem quite willing to play market prophet, given that if they are wrong, there is no one to drag them back on the air to try to explain their miscalculations to the poor saps who took their advice and got clobbered, certainly no one associated with the media that trotted them out as experts in the first place.

I've spent the better part of the last 20 years advising our clients and investors to think long term, but it's a challenge when they are continually bombarded by the media's so-called experts reporting on what's happening every five seconds. There is so much misinformation that investors would be better off watching

Rocky & Bullwinkle reruns — or better, the History Channel — than listening to the advice spewed by financial media's talking heads.

The media loves milestones, another excuse to obsess over an event or arbitrary number — 20,000, 25,000 or whatever — that has little or no relation to value aside from the context of earnings. At any indiscriminate number, the market may be overvalued or undervalued, just as purchasing a stock at $1 may be expensive while purchasing another at $10,000 may be cheap. These milestones do, however, bring out the pundits warning that stocks are certain to "plummet back to earth" or hyping some outrageously high number such as Dow 50,000. Either prediction is generally self-serving, designed principally for the so-called "experts" to shill for their new book or the financial products they are selling.

University of Texas professor Paul Tetlock quantitatively measured the interactions between the media and the stock market using daily content from a popular *Wall Street Journal* column. He found that high media pessimism predicts downward pressure on market prices followed by a reversion to fundamentals, and unusually high or low pessimism predicts high market trading volume. These and similar results are consistent with theoretical models of noise and liquidity traders, and are inconsistent with theories of media content as a proxy for new information about fundamental asset values.[26]

Finance is also a never-ending series of daily stories...increasingly dominated by the cacophony of voices, images, and events broadcast by television and online real-time data services. Finance has become a media event, with its breathless reporters and star anchorpersons more often approximating Entertainment Tonight or even (at the limit) MTV.[27]

In addition to the money managers — whether Bulls or Bears — appearing to promote their own self-interests, major investment bank analysts pop up with regularity to promote their agendas. Those whose research and information might actually be useful are the buy-side analysts, people working behind the scenes who make investment buying decisions for the bank's private clients, funds, and other internal accounts. Their knowledge is not for public consumption unless you subscribe to their research. These analysts are typically not the people who appear on the financial news, however; it is the sell-side analysts who do the heavy lifting for public consumption and the mass media. Sell-side analysts do what their name implies, they sell investment products, ostensibly by providing viewers with buy/sell recommendations they presumably believe in, but because they are pitching stocks or other investments for a reason — in some cases, because their firm's trading desk is wallowing in an issue they need to liquidate or distribute — their advice should be viewed with extreme skepticism.

As a rule, more advanced analytical skills and financial knowledge are required to become a buy-side analyst. One reason is that they are responsible for making investment decisions, as opposed to sell-side analysts whose primary requirements are communication skills and the ability to close the deal. The fact that buy-side analysts are considered more knowledgeable by their employers is adequate reason alone for you to question sell-side recommendations.

The darker side of financial news guests includes people like Henry Blodget, the quintessential example of a sell-side hustler. Blodget is a former equity research analyst for CIBC Oppenheimer and the head of the global Internet research team at Merrill Lynch during the dot-com era. His violations of securities laws resulted in his being banned for life from involvement in the securities industry.

His scandalous conduct included publicly touting certain internet stocks while privately describing them as "dogs" or "POS" (pieces of shit). He was fined $4 million and the SEC banned him for life from working in the financial services industry. That banishment didn't slow Henry up much or prevent him from becoming even wealthier in 2015, however, when he sold the financial news and gossip site he founded eight years previously for $343 million. Blodget is now a regular guest on CNBC and other financial news shows and blogs. Obviously, having a tarnished reputation is no obstacle to being sought out by an indiscriminate financial media purporting to provide their audience with "sound investment advice."

When I see investors flocking to get a piece of an IPO like Snapchat, following the advice of a sell-side analyst, I cringe. Granted, the company may eventually stop hemorrhaging money and find a way to monetize their business, but in the meantime, they are reliant on a youthful demographic known for its capriciousness and unpredictability.

I wonder how many investors would flock to buy stock in a company named Altrius if, as a sell-side analyst working for the IPO brokerage firm, I announced that the company expects to lose $3-4 million this year and next, but only $1-2 million the following year after which it anticipates becoming a permanently highly profitable company? That's exactly what sell-siders do; they emphasize a fledgling company's potential versus its actual value. The IPO price is most carefully chosen so as to avoid a premature drop. Investment banks don't want the stock to start at 20 and quickly drop to 15; they want a price that creates an immediate demand and rapidly escalates from 20 to 30 or 40 as the "excitement" builds and continues for as long as investors drink the Kool-Aid and the holding period expires. Yes, a few of these companies become viable but many without real earnings don't. Not to worry, the pitchmen will be back shortly with another exciting opportunity for you to get in on an IPO of a company losing money. And if that doesn't tickle your financial fancy, how about a hot stock currently trading at 50 to 100 times earnings with "unlimited growth potential?"

Today, when a money manager or analyst on TV recommends a stock, a disclaimer appears as to whether or not the person owns the stock, the idea being he is unbiased and has nothing to gain if he doesn't own it. But why should you buy a stock recommended by an analyst who doesn't own it himself? If it's so good, why isn't he buying it? It's reminiscent of advisors who sell annuities but who don't have any of their own money invested in them. They say annuities are good for their clients, but I would argue that they are much better for the brokers who receive a 6 or 7% commission for selling them.

I sometimes think there must be an obscure financial news employee with a Rolodex of potential talking heads labeled Optimists or Doomsayers. When the market tanks, they call up the doomsayers like David Stockman, the OMB "wunderkind" whose admitted "poor judgment and loose talk" damaged President Raegan's economic program. His continual proclamations that the market is about to descend into chaos, like a stopped clock, is right two seconds a day. He and other doomsday advocates, like Nouriel Roubini (aka Dr. Doom) become de rigueur talking heads when the market moves downward.

Don't expect to get substantive investment information from the pundits and assorted talking heads who appear on financial news shows. None of them know what the market is going to do tomorrow, next week or next year. They are on the air because the networks need to fill time so they can sell advertising. The guests are there to promote their agenda, business or latest book.

The media knows that men are psychologically wired to act, to do something. They deliver content with great excitement so as to make what they are saying sound more important than it is. That so many online trading services buy commercial time on these shows is indicative that advertisers have tapped into the same basic emotion. You have to resist the temptation to act. Turn off the TV. Sit on your hands. Take a walk. Read a book on economic history and educate yourself about finance without the talking head bias.

I'm often asked how I happen to know so much about a financial topic or historical economic event. The reason is simple: I read. Warren Buffett advised a class of graduating MBA's at Columbia University to read 500 pages a day. That's an ambitious schedule for someone running a business but I try to read 50-100 pages every day so I am educated on the topics that affect the financial lives of our clients. Wisdom isn't innate; it is acquired from reading continuously during a lifetime. It is this education of accumulated facts which shapes your brain into fertile soil from which to grow a productive crop to make educated investment decisions. Turn off your TV, cultivate an intellectual curiosity and read. We live in a time of unprecedented access to knowledge. Take advantage of it.

Importantly, the first thing you should do before you read anything is to investigate the author. Who's writing this and what's his bias? What's his agenda? Look the author up on Google. Find out all you can about him before you read what he has to say. One reason I enjoy reading what academics have to say is that in most cases, they are not selling anything, although they will still have a bias. The same holds true for me and this book. Learn to be a cynic.

> *"I find television very educating. Every time somebody turns on the set I go into the other room and read a book."*
> Groucho Marx

CHAPTER EIGHT

Biases: Politics, Religion and ESG

Does God want Aardvarks to be Rich?

We all have personal convictions and biases, whether they relate to politics, religion or social issues. The Constitution guarantees our right to be biased, whether right or wrong, but it's a mistake to base our investment decisions on our biases.

Politics

As a patriot, you can be concerned about the beliefs that form your political leanings. As a capitalist and investor, you can't let your political leanings influence your investment decisions.

Whether the White House is occupied by a Republican or Democrat has little effect on the number of hamburgers consumed in China. Money can be made regardless of the current administration, economic conditions or world events.

President Trump's election may have shocked the global financial markets, but despite the high levels of anxiety among many investors, a broad selloff never materialized. In fact, European and U.S. stocks quickly moved higher. Elections do not determine the long-term health of the economy or the businesses that operate within it.

Those who overreact to short-term events by making preemptive, emotionally charged investment decisions are more likely to be hurt than helped. Having the discipline to stay focused on the long-term drivers of investment performance is key to successful long-term investing.

I'm often asked which party is better for the economy and to which party I belong. As to the latter question, I generally quip that I am a Federalist and my party died with Hamilton's demise on the banks of Weehawken, New Jersey. To the former question, I believe that though elections are of vital importance to the direction of our nation, the person elected has little long-term impact on our resilient American economy.

As a patriot, I am concerned about political matters and the important issues of our time. As a capitalist, however, I don't let my political opinions influence our investments as I understand that innovative companies will thrive somewhere in our global economy. As I often state at our investment committee meetings, "What impact does an election have on how much Nestle chocolate is consumed in Latin America or Pepsi Colas drunk in Africa or India?"

My friend Todd Young, with whom I went to school at the Naval Academy and served in the Marine Corps, was elected Senator from Indiana in 2017. As much as I believe strongly in Todd's honor, intelligence, and passion to serve our country, his election will, in reality, have little long-term impact on the global earnings of the companies in which we are invested.

"I am quite sure now that often, in matters concerning religion and politics, a man's reasoning powers are not above the monkey's."
Mark Twain

The handwringing and worry associated with political elections can cause investors to make foolish decisions which are harmful to their health and wealth. For this reason, I recommend investors remain calm during election periods. Avoid watching news channels as study after study has displayed that investors perform poorly when acting on short-term news. Better to enjoy a good economic or history book, or if you must, to at least enjoy the political season for the circus it is!

Socially Responsible Investing

Socially responsible investing (SRI) can be defined as an investment that is considered socially responsible because of the nature of the business the company conducts.[28]

I believe SRI is a grey, highly individualized area that purports to achieve the impossible: to determine that one company be deemed "good" with another "evil" based upon varied factors such as a few individuals, methodologies, operational procedures, business practices or the product(s) sold. Those who tout SRI and ESG (environmental, social, and governance) strategies are either disingenuous but understand it is a great marketing gimmick, or are simply clouded by their own biases, believing theirs is the "right" cause of action under which all investing decisions should flow.

To me, applying a prism of particular SRI or ESG filters is inconsistent with a fiduciary responsibility to achieve the best possible return for our clients. That said, I believe that companies which take a long-term approach and act ethically will best be able to create more sustainable and profitable businesses due to the trust they've built over time. Even a company that creates something which someone may deem as "evil" (possibly tobacco manufacturers or technology companies attempting to addict us to our screens), should be open and transparent about what they do in selling the product they are producing. As a money manager, my mandate is to provide the best risk-adjusted rate of return possible for our clients. Investment analysis requires tremendous amounts of study and experience to make a reasoned determination on whether or not to invest in a particular company. Adding the complexities of the percentage of green buildings, women in management and the board's diversity (not to mention which percentage is acceptable) pushes one into very grey determinants encumbered by complicated concepts.

As to whether or not socially responsible investing — or environmental, social, and governance — provides better returns, I believe the jury is still out. Those who purport that it does continue to promote it. Even those who may not have a direct skin in the game, such as professors at academic institutions, are likely biased by their viewpoints on such issues as climate change, diversity, consumer protection, animal welfare and the like.

Writing in *Pension Management*, author Jack Gray argues that "Boards spend excessive time on ESG relative to any expected benefits for the principals...or its potential to improve member's returns." Gray also holds that "ESG investors risk overpaying for the 'privilege' of owning them, almost regardless of price."[29]

"There is one and only one social responsibility of business — to use its resources and engage in activities designed to increase its profits so long as it stays within the rules of the game, which is to say, engages in open and free competition without deception or fraud."

Milton Friedman

I agree with the author that most boards are ill-equipped to determine what companies are ESG friendly. Those that believe they can are either naïve or duplicitous. As he points out, executives are masters at "listening inactivity, a core competency they develop from explaining themselves to hordes of analysts and portfolio managers." This is why I don't waste my time listening to earnings calls wherein self-serving analysts, typically from the big investment banks, ask silly questions to which everyone knows the answers, or to make themselves sound important.

Writing on SRI for cbsnews.com, columnist Larry Swedroe notes that "SRI funds are typically more expensive than index funds and passive funds in general. One reason is that they incur the extra costs of screening out the undesirables. Those extra costs can hurt returns. SRI investors also typically sacrifice diversification as SRI funds are often domestic and large cap. Thus, investors sacrifice exposure to small-cap and value stocks, and perhaps international, and emerging market stocks as well. They also then lose exposure to the higher expected returns provided by small-cap, value, and emerging market stocks. SRI investors also may be accepting other risks. Because they avoid investing is "sin" stocks, they're not fully diversified across industries."[30]

According to bizfluent.com, Corporate Social Responsibility (CSR) often requires changes to a number of processes, as well as increased reporting. In many cases, businesses hire additional personnel to manage CSR initiatives. These actions may come at a cost, and opponents point out that the money spent on CSR comes directly from shareholders' pockets. Former investment banker and current Tulane University professor Elaine Sternberg, one of the most vocal opponents of the effects of CSR on shareholder profits, points out that CSR initiatives incur great cost with little measurable return.[31]

I don't make political or moral judgments about a company unless a client asks us to blacklist a particular company or industry due to one or more of their strongly held beliefs. For one, things are rarely black and white. For example, if the Gates Foundation gives to Planned Parenthood but Microsoft doesn't, does that mean we can invest in Microsoft or we can't? Secondly, the judgements on the gradation of a company's product or service are extremely complex — not to mention the time and cost of doing so. Is soda harmful? How about diet soda? If it is, to what extent and how much must be consumed for it to be harmful? Just as with personal politics, I advise you not to let a company's politics influence your investment choices.

Where Does It Stop?

I was illustrating this point to my son who had asked about coal. I showed him an economic map that revealed how the coal mines and rail lines intersect along the Appalachian Mountains. I then showed him the income statement of a railway company. He saw that coal represents a significant portion of their cargo and that the company lost billions of dollars over the last few years because of the decline in coal prices. Unfortunately, we can't light up a large city grid with renewable energy sources like solar energy yet. Thus, we still have to use gas and coal fired plants to power our nation — particularly since there remains a tremendous amount of fear regarding nuclear energy. Should an investor take a position that he won't invest in coal companies? Does that mean we also can't invest in the rail companies because they generate revenue from coal as well? Does that mean that we can't own utility companies because they're using coal to fire up their plants? If you have a prohibition against one particular issue, where does it stop?

The same holds true for environmental, social, and governance (ESG). Who determines what percentage of women on a company's board achieves adequate diversification? Who's to say that the things I believe in will be beneficial to society and therefore provide a better investment return?

Don't let yourself get sucked into thinking that social investing will deliver a better return. There are lots of companies selling grading classifications that somehow determine one company is green and worth investing in and another company isn't...or that this company has better social governance than this company. They love to cite individual situations to support their position, such as the reason why a particular board blew up is because it didn't take "proper human resources policies" into consideration. How do you get inside a company to make those determinations? If activist private equity firms and hedge funds with board seats have had limited to no influence on improving profitability, sometimes doing so by spearheading ESG efforts, how can an individual investor or institutional investment board of a foundation expect to do so?

To me, these issues are exceptionally subjective. Whether it's environmental, social, or governance scores, it's really the opinion of someone entering data into a computer and making subjective (and sometimes moral) judgments in hazy areas with limited internal knowledge of complex circumstances.

I'm completely agnostic toward ESG issues. I prefer to look at the numbers of the company and its potential. When meeting with company executives to determine qualitative data, I'm doing so to explore whether these are good businesspeople who are going to pay back the money we lend them. Good management is honest and understands that good governance naturally flows when ethical leadership and long-term profit seeking measures are aligned.

This is why I don't believe in activist investing and instead simply invest in good companies that I want to hold long term. Should I invest in a distressed issue, I am doing so because the price is cheap and I believe that the current or future management will eventually improve the sales and profitability of the company.

> *I saw my six-year-old daughter watching "The Lorax," a movie based on the Dr. Seuss story. Although the Lorax character was ostensibly used to express Dr. Seuss' anger at corporate greed, it also shows that greed and care of the environment can coincide with one another.*
>
> *Another fictional Seuss character, the Once-ler, is depicted as a faceless green suit that in his greed and blindness destroys an entire ecosystem in order to create a product called a "Thneed".[32] If the Once-ler cuts down all of the Truffula trees to make Thneeds, his business will eventually go bankrupt. He may be able to make profits in the short term, but if he wants to be profitable over the long term, he must be a caretaker and responsibly cultivate the growth of the Truffula trees so as to not wind up telling a sad story among a barren land.*

Religion

There are numerous faith-based funds associated with various religious groups. Religious affinity investments represent billions of dollars. One financial advisor in the Atlanta area with billions under management offers "Principles-Based Investing combining a deep understanding of timeless biblical truths" according to its website. While the majority of these funds and strategies reflect the values of the religious groups they purport to represent, it wouldn't take much effort to append a couple of bible verses onto almost any investment principle and declare one is a bible-based advisor promoting prosperity through faith. Though I thought long and hard during many periods of my life about a calling to the priesthood, I would never feel comfortable building my business by using religion as a marketing plan.

For one, I understand that I am an imperfect man incapable of living up to perfect ideals. I wouldn't want my clients and friends to entrust their assets to our firm with an expectation that I will not make mistakes in my life and potentially become disillusioned by my missteps. Secondly, I don't know if God wants us to be financially successful or not. The ideals I've studied for endeavoring to live a noble life have little connection with monetary things and many, like St. Francis and Mother Teresa, have lived with little worldly possessions while leaving a remarkable legacy. Faith, hope, and charity require a belief in the Divine while the cardinal virtues of prudence, temperance, fortitude, and justice may be well exemplified by non-believers alike.

Though falling short daily, I attempt to apply the cardinal virtues in my life, coupled with our firm's Guiding Principles of Integrity, Humility, Competence, and Compassion. I was also profoundly impacted by my time at the Naval Academy, inculcating our Honor Code that a Midshipman will not lie, cheat or steal. Though our firm has been built on a foundation of trust over the past two decades, I remind our associates often that we can ruin that trust with just one lie or worse, an act of thievery.

CNBC's "American Greed" series features a number of episodes about religious investment scams, many of which revolve around an advisor involved with a church. The trusting nature of many religious worshippers, and, often, their fervent wish to help others, have opened the floodgates to the evil deception of the church scam. Others, like Bernie Madoff, scammed many in the Jewish community.

Church scams can happen when members of a congregation, a church, temple or mosque, or even a whole religious organization, are fooled into parting with their money either for a supposedly profitable investment or simply to support an individual who claims to have fallen on hard times.

Tens of millions of dollars have been plowed by individuals into hopeless projects that have turned out to be Ponzi schemes.[33]

One Ponzi scheme promoter sold promissory notes bearing purported annual interest rates of 12% to 20%, telling primarily African-American investors that the funds would be used to purchase and support small businesses such as a laundry, juice bar or gas station. The promoter also sold "sweepstakes machines" that he claimed would generate investor returns of as much as 300% or more in the first year.

Self-proclaimed "Social Capitalist" and former CEO of City Capital Corporation Ephren W. Taylor, II operated a Ponzi scheme to swindle over $11 million, primarily from African-American churchgoers. To tap into the investors' largest source of available funds, Taylor encouraged investors to roll-over retirement portfolios to self-directed IRA custodial accounts, which he facilitated, and then invest those funds with Taylor and City Capital. In reality, City Capital never generated significant – if any – revenue from actual business operations, but instead was wholly dependent upon a continuous stream of new investor funds just to stay open. When new investor funds dried up during the latter half of 2010, the entire operation ground to a halt, leaving hundreds of swindled investors.[34]

Another Ponzi scheme in Dallas, TX raised almost $6 million from nearly 80 evangelical Christian investors through fraudulent, unregistered offerings of stock and short-term, high-yield promissory notes issued by their company, which was marketed as a voice-over-internet-protocol video services provider around the world.

On April 30, 2012, the SEC filed settled fraud charges against the company, alleging that owners Terry and Scott Wiese promised extreme returns – as much as 1,000% in a year – to entice investment in their company, Usee, Inc. Contrary to the Wieses' claims, however, Usee had no business from which to generate any returns to investors. Instead, the Commission alleges that the Wieses wasted investor funds on poorly considered ventures or sent them to third parties about which they had little information. The Commission also alleges that the Wieses used investor funds for personal expenses and to make Ponzi payments to investors.[35]

As with social or political predilections, I advise investors to not let those preferences cloud their investment decisions. Instead, I recommend donating to the charities and causes they feel most strongly about from their income or the profits from their investments.

Regardless of a company's environmental, social, religious, political or governance positions, I'm not going to invest in it if I don't like their fundamentals, their business or their growth potential. I'm perfectly content to let the executives who are closest to the business make the decisions to best guide the company as their incentives are generally aligned with shareholders. Should they not do so, the board and shareholders will eventually find a management team capable to make the requisite changes for the company to remain in business and eventually grow again.

I don't get involved in activism because I don't believe it is time well spent or impactful on performance. Like the aardvark, we know there are certain things to be aware of, such as predators out there trying to eat you. On the other hand, there are things you can't let bother you, like the weather. Whether it's the hot sun or the driving rain, you can't let it prevent you from getting out there and finding what you need, understanding that the noise coming from political, religious, environmental, social or governance issues are mostly inconsequential to the long-term profits of a company.

"You call my candidate a horse thief, and I call yours a lunatic, and we both of us know it's just till election day. It's an American custom, like eating corn on the cob. And, afterwards, we settle down quite peaceably and agree we've got a pretty good country - until next election."

Stephen Vincent Benet

Section II

Investing Like an Aardvark

CHAPTER NINE

Value

Digging Deep, Alone and Unafraid

I believe that value investing involves selecting stocks that trade for less than their intrinsic value. As a value investor, I refuse to pay more for a security than I believe it's worth, confident that over time, the market will reward the intrinsic value inherent in the security. It's often very hard to be a value investor: like the aardvark, we are contrarian creatures by nature.

As a value investor, I refuse to chase momentum. One reason I recommend that you not do so is highlighted in a research paper published in the *Financial Analysts Journal* which reports that a large body of empirical research indicates that value stocks, on average, earn higher returns than growth stocks. The sharp rise and subsequent decline during the late 1990's and early 2000's of technology and other growth-oriented stocks also calls into question the argument that growth stocks are better investments than value stocks. In addition to potentially higher returns, the evidence from a variety of indicators, including beta and return volatility, suggests that value stocks are also less risky than growth stocks. Indeed, based on mathematical risk indicators that focus on performance in down markets, value stocks suffered less severely than growth stocks when the stock market or the overall economy did poorly.

The superior performance of value stocks cannot be attributed to their risk exposure. A more convincing explanation for the value premium (the spread in returns between value and growth stocks identified by famed academics Fama and French as one of the three factors in their asset pricing model) rests on characteristics of investor behavior. As an example, during the tech bubble of the late 1990's and early 2000's (as was the case in numerous past episodes in financial history), investors extrapolated from the past and became excessively excited about promising new technologies. They overbid the prices of apparent growth stocks while the prices of value stocks dropped far below their value based on fundamentals. Because these behavioral traits will probably continue to exist in the future, patient investing in value stocks is likely to remain a rewarding long-term investment strategy.[36]

The aardvark doesn't chase critters it can't digest.

A Good Question

Recently, a client asked the good question of why we would purchase a company which has declined in value — while selling or trimming our positions in companies which have risen in price.

Here's my response to his inquiry:

> *Yours is a good question, one asked not only by our clients, but also by advisors to whom we sell and my own analysts and financial advisors since we all tend to focus on the worst performing stocks in the short term. Of note, I'm wired a bit differently (ask my wife) and actually prefer for stocks to go down in value so I can purchase more shares at cheaper values. Though I get paid less when the market declines since our fees are based upon portfolio value, our clients' income doesn't change as long as the dividend remains stable and/or continues to grow.*

I like to invest in companies I'm comfortable owning for a long period of time, companies whose business I would like to own — not thinking simply as owning shares of a stock, but as a business owner.

My process is a Three Prong Strategy which entails purchasing companies that have these characteristics:

1. **Value**: selling for a reasonable or distressed valuation below what I believe to be its intrinsic value;

2. **Dividends**: Growing and generally above average dividends, and;

3. **Global Macro**: having potential for earnings and revenue growth both domestically and abroad. In addition to the micro, this characteristic also includes a macro framework in which I may find value in certain geographic areas of growth or a sector/industry which I believe to be undervalued.

Within the Value framework, I purchase companies which fall into three categories:

1. **Classic Value**: Companies which usually sell for lower valuations and contain higher dividends, such as financials, health care, energy, etc. This category typically comprises the largest amount of our portfolio unless we are in a recession;

2. **Persistent Earners**: Companies which are selling below their historical valuations and are reasonably priced while also exhibiting steadier, more reliable earnings over time in good and bad markets. This category is generally the second largest in our portfolio as we are usually unable or unwilling to purchase richly valued companies — unless the entire market has sold off driving valuations down for everyone or the sector, or company, has experienced a decline; and

3. **Distressed/Contrarian**: Companies everyone hates and continue to sell, exacerbating price declines. Due to the volatility in this category, it's almost always the smallest portion of our portfolio. This category can include companies that have tremendous gains when the consensus is wrong on them, but also may include companies that are actually going out of business. Though Warren Buffett is now too large to invest in such companies, he used to do so often, calling them "cigar butts." They are companies which have been thrown out but still have a few puffs of smoke in them. The stub may be ugly and soggy but it's still producing some smoke (revenue) and may have value left. Though buying companies under their book value is effectively impossible since the Great Depression, the theory on purchasing such "tossed away" companies remains the same.

The aardvark hunts alone, at night, when other predators are sleeping.

More Art Than Science

There is of course no mathematical formula for which one can produce an algorithm with the above metrics to spit out companies in which to invest. Thus, there is more art than science employed when purchasing any company I decide to invest in, understanding that I could screen out every available company if I wanted it to fit perfectly into my investment process. The process merely acts as a framework for which to make decisions. If I believe that the company's prospects are sound for a turnaround over the long term (5-10 years), I will invest.

From a philosophical standpoint, why would one want to pay more rather than less for an asset? Doing so would be akin to regularly swapping homes in an expensive neighborhood, paying more each time for your neighbors' house. Our alternative approach would be to sell your well appreciated home in your expensive neighborhood and move to a neighborhood that provides the same shelter and comforts (hopefully in an up and coming area) and ideally, purchasing a multi-family home to live on one side while having the other half of the home provide rental income (dividends) on which you may live while the homes fluctuate in value. The deepest type of distressed/value investing is going into dilapidated/burned out neighborhoods, believing a revitalization will occur as a city's population pushes further out into the suburbs. This is obviously riskier — while also entailing more patience and time.

I believe, and many academic studies have confirmed, that value investing outperforms with less risk over time as measured by common mathematical formulas such as beta or standard deviation. Graphic 9.1 supports my contention.

The chart illustrates that over the past six decades, the lowest P/E stocks delivered an average annual return of 12.99%, significantly outperforming the highest P/E stocks at 8.50%, as well as other, higher P/E stocks and the S&P 500 index. The lowest P/E stocks also displayed lower volatility — as measured by the average annual standard deviation — than the highest P/E stocks by roughly 15% (16.45 vs 19.40). These figures are rarely discussed on the financial news shows that prefer to focus on high-flying momentum stocks with sky-high P/E ratios.

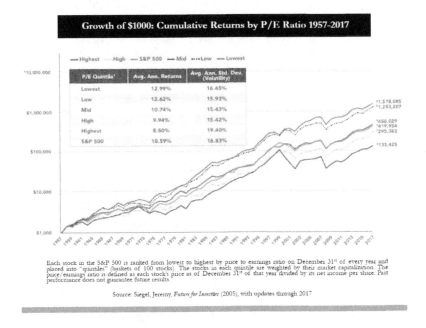

Growth of $1000: Cumulative Returns by P/E Ratio 1957-2017

— Highest · · · · High — S&P 500 — Mid · · · ·Low — Lowest

P/E Quintile[1]	Avg. Ann. Returns	Avg. Ann. Std. Dev. (Volatility)
Lowest	12.99%	16.45%
Low	12.62%	15.93%
Mid	10.74%	15.43%
High	9.94%	15.42%
Highest	8.50%	19.40%
S&P 500	10.59%	16.83%

Each stock in the S&P 500 is ranked from lowest to highest by price to earnings ratio on December 31st of every year and placed into "quintiles" (baskets of 100 stocks). The stocks in each quintile are weighted by their market capitalization. The price/earnings ratio is defined as each stock's price as of December 31st of that year divided by its net income per share. Past performance does not guarantee future results.

Source: Siegel, Jeremy, *Future for Investors* (2005), with updates through 2017

Fig. 9.1 Returns by P/E Ratio

Though these mathematical equations provide some value, it is important to understand that I don't believe risk should be measured in a mathematical manner. Ultimately, risk should be measured based upon the probability of a company's demise over the long term —— and can only be measured after the fact. Thus, risk is something which I believe can't be measured; it's art that requires experience and time to determine an appropriate value for a security. It's why I sometimes think people with philosophy degrees are better at investing than the mathematicians, who almost blew the world up a decade ago and are still making decisions based upon highly imperfect models.

One Man's Growth is Another Man's Value

Many who call themselves value managers buy companies at their highest valuation, claiming they are cheap. They believe stocks can overcome high valuations (as measured by price to earnings ratio or other calculation) with strong growth.

Don't be fooled by these imposters. They are growth managers disguised as value managers, often using the price/earnings to growth ratio (PEG) made famous by Peter Lynch at Fidelity and regularly touted by pundits like CNBC's Jim Cramer to promote sexy growth stocks.

The problem with applying a particular growth ratio to a company is knowing what growth rate to use. Will it continue to grow at its current level or is the market saturated? Is the company selling a fad product that will quickly fade once teenage girls grow bored with it?

As a company grows, its growth rate will eventually slow due to the law of large numbers. The most successful companies — even those with a monopolistic position experiencing tremendous expansion — will ultimately have their growth rate revert to the mean. Thus, describing a company selling at one hundred times earnings and growing at 50% per year (PEG ratio of 100/50 or 2) as a "value" company is a misnomer in my opinion. I believe using more traditional valuation metrics — such as price to earnings or cash flow — and assuming more realistic growth valuations over a longer period of time are better methods to avoid overpaying for a company, and provide a purer definition of value.

The popular show *Shark Tank* offers a good metaphor of how to define value. Willing only to pay for real past earnings, the sharks refuse to apply an exorbitant multiple (price to earnings ratio) to companies being pitched to them. The sharks invest their money in a disciplined manner, understanding that it will take time to recoup their initial investment before beginning to participate in potential future earnings.

Investing in a stock should be conducted with similar discipline. Just as the sharks aren't willing to invest based purely on potential, neither should you invest in a company promising great potential but lacking real earnings or selling at an unreasonably high valuation.

Don't also make the mistake of thinking a company is cheap because it is selling at $1 or that it is expensive because it is selling for $1,000. The price of the stock is irrelevant. To determine value, consider the price in relation to its earnings while applying a realistic growth potential. An "expensive" stock can be cheap and a "cheap" stock expensive. Those unwisely investing in penny stocks with no earnings quickly realize this error. A company producing no income after expenses is simply one in the process of going bankrupt. Investing in such penny stocks is an exercise of hoping another sucker buys it to drive the price higher and that you exit before you are the last sucker holding the bag when the music stops.

Beware the frenzy surrounding a stock split. When a company decides to split its stock, it adds no value as its earnings remain exactly the same. Investors tend to get excited when a company's stock splits — solely for that event — without understanding that it was the underlying fundamentals of earnings growth which enabled the split to occur. On the opposite side of the spectrum, I had a client blame his former company's reverse split (the stock's price was increased and shares reduced) for the company's demise when, in reality, the company's fall was due to a deterioration of earnings wherein the stock price naturally also fell.

Over longer periods of time, stock prices will eventually follow a company's earnings. In the short term, investors can drive a price to dizzying heights based upon the excitement of its growth potential, or conversely, to lower lows due to abject fear about its prospects. A value investor can take advantage of such negative sentiment as the price has been driven to a low valuation because selling begat more selling as investors believed the company's prospects greatly diminished. A value investor must be contrarian by nature, and though it often doesn't feel right to invest when others are selling, significant bargains can be found if you are willing to bravely step up when others have given up.

A Sheep in Wolf's Clothing

The discrepancy between a mutual fund's marketing description and its investment process often leads to a confusing moniker. William H. Miller, who served as the chairman and chief investment officer of Legg Mason Capital Management, was also the principal portfolio manager of the (misnamed) Legg Mason Capital Management Value Trust.

Miller, who considered himself a value investor, constructed portfolios under the value label that (according to his 2006 letter to shareholders) contained "a mix of companies whose fundamental valuation factors differ. We have high P/E and low P/E, high price-to-book and low-price-to-book. We differ from many value investors in being willing to analyze stocks that look expensive to see if they really are. Most, in fact, are, but some are not. To the extent we get that right, we will benefit shareholders and clients."[37] To one clearly looking at what he said, I would assert that Miller likes to purchase both growth and value stocks. Benjamin Graham, who was Warren Buffett's professor at Columbia and wrote *The Intelligent Investor*, the bible for value investors, would likely roll over in his grave with such a definition of value investing.

I honestly don't know how anyone can regard Miller as a value investor. He certainly had a remarkable run, beating the S&P 500 for 15 consecutive years ending in 2005. However, the fund began a downward spiral with huge losses due to large bets on hobbled financial stocks during the financial crisis, according to Morningstar. After a decade of performance near the absolute bottom of his peer group, performance which horrifically trailed the S&P 500, Miller suffered an ignominious end when he departed the fund in 2016. Miller's amorphous fund certainly didn't employ a value strategy as it was crammed with growth and momentum stocks at ridiculous multiples.

I believe that value investing should stick to a purer valuation metric as study after academic study has shown that traditional valuation methods work when valuing a company. Burton Malkiel's classic book on finance, *A Random Walk Down Wall Street*, had a profound impact on me over two decades ago. Malkiel, a professor of economics at Princeton University, debunks most of the investing schemes which have been attempted over the years with the one notable exception of recognizing that lower P/E companies outperform higher multiple stocks (i.e. growth stocks). Though considering many valuation metrics (such as cash flow, book value, etc.) when analyzing the puzzle pieces of a particular investment opportunity, I find myself often utilizing the P/E ratio as my primary consideration, one that usually presents the clearest — albeit most traditional — definition of value.

Staying on the Savanna When the Weather is Terrible

Though over the past decade, value investing has had its longest period of underperformance in relation to growth since the 1930's, I believe that over time, value investing is superior to chasing momentum and paying for growth at any price. Value investing often takes great patience to wait for an investment to reach its intrinsic value — sometimes years of feeling you are the only person left on earth believing a particular company is a sound investment. During such periods, managers who work for large financial firms might be fired for underperformance and relative losses against a particular index. It takes tremendous fortitude to stick with such an investment, and even more to purchase more shares when it continues to decline with short sellers swirling. In recent years post the financial crisis, many have looked for a means to dampen market volatility leading to a proliferation of long-short strategies. These strategies combine buying high-priced momentum stocks fueling further price appreciation coupled with shorting declining stocks which drives them even lower. The strategies are further exacerbated in today's algorithmically-driven trading environment and can quickly make a value investor purchasing low-priced stocks feel very foolish.

Yet, this is exactly the type of grit and endurance necessary to be successful as a value investor. In my opinion, risk cannot be accurately measured by a mathematical formula calculating volatility from a mean. Instead, risk should be considered from the potential failure of the company over the long term. When confronted with a stock declining in value which no one believes in, I find it important to focus on the goods or product the company is selling, asking yourself if you believe that product will never be purchased by consumers again. If the answer is no, then don't worry about the price of the stock in the short term, particularly when the company is priced at exceptionally low valuations. Turn off the television and instead focus on the longer-term prospects of the company, and the fact that it will take management time to turn operations around. It will better enable you stay invested in the company.

I certainly cannot guarantee that value investing will outperform growth and momentum investing as it has in the past. I will, however, argue that value investing will, at the least, better protect your portfolio from suffering catastrophic failure when overvalued companies eventually fall back to reality.

The Danger of Running with the (Growth) Herd

As I write this chapter, former tech darling GoPro has reported it is laying off another 20% of its workforce and the stock has fallen almost 20% today. This is yet another example of the dangers of investing in a company with unrealistic growth expectations and what happens when they don't materialize. The company IPO'd at $24 in 2014 and hit a high of about $80, flying higher on hope of continued growth. Prior to the beginning of its collapse in 2015, roughly 70% of Wall Street analysts maintained a buy rating, none with a sell or strong sell.

The fear of missing out (FOMO) is very strong on such companies when they go public or reach new highs. Maintaining the discipline to not pay too much for a company and not purchasing companies that don't provide income to our clients kept me from purchasing GoPro, among the many other growth companies which have failed. Though value investing also entails suffering through such declines at times, and entails the risks of "catching a falling knife," time has proven that patient value investors like me are able to purchase such companies at more reasonable valuations and achieve sound risk-adjusted returns over time. Though you may not be able to brag to your golf buddies about the hot, highflying stock you purchased, maintaining this patient discipline may help you stay in the fairway and win the more important score in the clubhouse.

For every one company that defies the odds of high valuations by achieving long term success, there are more GoPro's which fail miserably at worst and provide horrific returns at best. Your golfing friends won't mention these stocks which likely created greater losses than the one stock that provided some gains — just as they won't count that mulligan!

Though raging bull markets will continue to be driven by growth stocks (especially in today's passive/index driven world in which the largest market cap companies become even larger), eventually, bear markets occur and I believe it is then, as in the past, that my value approach of purchasing cheaper/lower beta stocks better enables us to not lose as much during the inevitable sell offs of growth stocks when expectations don't materialize.

As a value investor, I resist overpaying for ridiculously valued companies that lure investors in with their momentum. So many have made the mistake of jumping into investments that were the fad of the day for fear of missing out.

As we used to say with our NATOPS (Naval Air Training and Operating Procedures Standardization) manual, there are some procedures which are written in blood and if you chase momentum, you will eventually blow yourself up. Like the inviolate rules when I flew C130s, there are certain things I believe you should never do when investing. The euphoria of the masses may make it seem as though you can go ahead and do it at the time, but like unwary pilots, investors can get killed.

Investment Managers Often Hunt Big Game

Mistakes chasing momentum are not limited to individual or even institutional investors. Some of the most widely heralded managers have fallen prey.

When long-time Fidelity manager George Vanderheiden was forced into resigning, Karen Firestone took over the reins of the Fidelity's Destiny I fund.

Under Vanderheiden, the Destiny I fund had returned 19.3% annually from 1980 through his departure in 2000, an admirable record. But when value stocks temporarily fell out of favor during the tech, internet, and growth stock run up in the late 90's, Vanderheiden refused to join the stampede and was ultimately replaced. Apparently, Fidelity believed that he didn't understand "this time was different" and that "internet stocks are the future."

According to a 2000 *New York Times* article, "Mr. Vanderheiden said he thought a value revival might be just around the corner, noting that the end of other investing crazes — the run-up in the Japanese stock market during the 1980's, the biotechnology craze of 1991 and the rise of the Nifty 50 in 1972 — all fizzled around the start of a new year. 'What I've found over a lot of years is that a lot of these manias seem to end at the end of the year'."[38]

Vanderheiden had it dead right. Firestone, on the other hand, had no hesitation plunging the fund into tech stocks, just in time for the tech bubble to burst. Firestone, who worked under Peter Lynch since 1983, should have known better. She later admitted as much in her 2016 book, "Even the Odds."

> *"2000 and 2001 were really gut-wrenching. In a personal sense, I felt worse in 2000, because there were so many signs of a bubble. My predecessor on Destiny Fund, George Vanderheiden, was so right that this tech bubble was going to burst. He had gotten out of those stocks in 1998," Firestone said. When she took over, it was tough to stay out of tech stocks at the risk of falling behind the competition in a go-go market. But the downdraft was painful. "I really felt as if I should have known better in 2000."* [39]

Of course, due to her pedigree, wealthy investors were willing to overlook her blunders and, incredibly, trusted her with $1.4 billion after she cofounded her own firm in 2005. I recently heard her touting growth stocks on CNBC, once again chasing performance. Evidently, neither she nor her investors have learned the lessons of the past.

Warren Buffett has some deceptively simple rules that underpin his value investment approach. I subscribe to them and I believe you would do well to do the same. Here are a few golden Buffett nuggets regarding value investing:

- ✓ Always invest for the long term.
- ✓ Whether we're talking about socks or stocks, I like buying quality merchandise when it is marked down.
- ✓ Buy a business, don't rent stocks.
- ✓ If you don't feel comfortable owning something for 10 years, then don't own it for 10 minutes.
- ✓ Price is what you pay. Value is what you get.

CHAPTER TEN

Dependable Dividends

Eating Ants Isn't Sexy, but it Provides Sound Sustenance

As a rule, I don't invest in companies that don't pay a dividend as I like to "get paid to wait" while patiently owning companies for the long term.

Dividends have long been an important source of returns for investors and a way for companies to share profits in a predictable manner. But while majority owners of companies have discretionary access to the cash and assets of a firm, individual investors have no way of unlocking value from an investment except through dividends, company liquidation, or selling to a future higher bidder.

In an era of aging demographics, dividends are likely to play an increasingly important role. Dividends better align the interests of management and stockholders while also offering and favorable tax treatment.

As graphic 10.1 illustrates, high dividend yielding stocks have tended to outperform over long time horizons, furthering the case for focusing on dividends as a fundamental metric for assessing investments.

"The greatest of all gifts is the power to estimate things at their true worth."
François de La Rochefoucauld

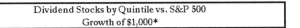

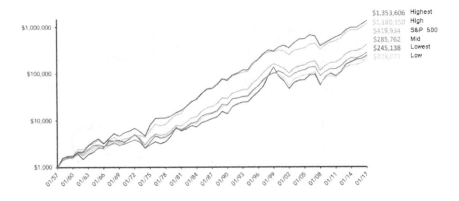

*Source: Siegel, Jeremy, *Future for Investors* (2005), with updates through 2017
ı "What do dividends tell us about earnings quality," Douglas Skinner, Chicago Booth School of Business

Fig.10.1 Dividend Stocks by Quintile

You may notice the relative performance similarity of high dividend yield stocks to that of stocks with the lowest P/E ratios (graphic 9.1 in the previous chapter). It's no coincidence.

According to some academic theories, such as Modigliani and Miller's "dividend irrelevance" theorem, whether earnings are retained, spent on stock repurchases, or distributed as dividends should have no impact on shareholder value, as investors could effectively replicate these events through buying and selling shares on the open market.[40] In a theoretical world without informational and transactional frictions, this theory appears plausible. In the real world, however, dividends may add value by reducing agency costs of asymmetric information, improving the reliability of accounting estimates, and signaling future prospects.

Asymmetric information can lead to conflicts of interest wherein policies which benefit management may not be in the best interest of shareholders, such as the use of extra company funds to splurge on private jets or lavish networking events. A dividend policy can help to align interests by directing resources toward maintaining and growing dividends rather than increasing management benefits and power.

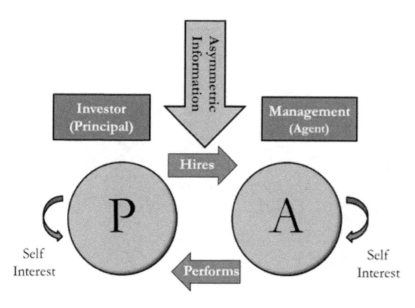

Fig. 10.2 Asymmetric Info

Management can smooth earnings by postponing or accelerating the recognition of revenues and expenses, but unlike estimates of earnings, cash flows, and the value of assets on a balance sheet, a dividend check is impossible to fake or manipulate. A truly profitable ongoing business venture should generate cash flows that can be distributed as an assurance of its fundamental earnings power. Supporting this, a 2009 University of Chicago/Harvard University study found that earnings consistency from year to year was greater for firms that paid dividends.[41]

Dividend Signaling

Dividends may act as a signal into what management expects the future of a company to look like. Since company insiders presumably have superior insight into business conditions, this signaling effect can impact the degree to which investors feel comfortable about long-term investments. Even if a company is going through a temporarily difficult time financially, management may have visibility into future changes that will restore profitability, reducing cash flow concerns. A dividend cut can be interpreted as a potential red flag concerning the earnings power of the business model.

This effect can be observed empirically in the reaction of stock prices to changes in dividend policy. A 2011 Harvard/NYU study documented a difference in price reaction to surprise dividend cuts of roughly twice the magnitude of the reaction to similar dividend raises.[42] This implies that investors are risk-averse and concerned about the future implications of cuts.

Dividends versus Share Repurchases

A 2000 study by Fama and French documented the decline of dividends and rise in share repurchases, showing that the proportion of US-listed firms paying dividends declined from 67% in 1978 to 21% in 2000.[43] In many cases, dividends were replaced by an increase in stock buybacks, under the argument that the methods are theoretically equivalent.

In practice, executives often appear to buy stock at the wrong time, perhaps overpaying for shares. When stock prices are low, a business is usually struggling, liquidity is important, and its credit rating may be at risk. Management, therefore, is likely to repurchase shares only when they are fully or overvalued by the market.

Changing Investor Preferences

Just as companies go through different phases in the business cycle, so too do investors go through lifecycle changes and times when they prefer different types of returns. These changes can be influenced by age, health, tax status, employment, sentiment, or any of a number of other variables.

A 2004 article by Baker and Wurgler proposed a "Catering Theory of Dividends," wherein managers pay dividends when investors place a premium in the stock market on companies that do so.[44] The idea is that dividends go in and out of style depending on the time period. They found that managers do tend to initiate dividends when investors place a relatively higher value on payers while tending to omit them when nonpayers are preferred.

Further research in an article by King Fuei Lee demonstrated that periods with high dividend premiums were associated with changes in the ratio of older to younger members of the population.[45] Essentially, the more people entering old age relative to youths, the higher the premium placed on the stock prices of dividend-payers.

Even as investor preferences gravitate toward a stable-return, yield-focused approach to investing, corporations have never been better positioned to raise dividends. Capital gains no longer receive preferential tax treatment, eliminating a major argument for retaining earnings (see graphic 10.3). US corporations have over $2 trillion in idle cash, twice what they have historically held as a percentage of capital expenditures. Companies are running lean from technological innovation and cost-cutting through the recent years of tight credit conditions.

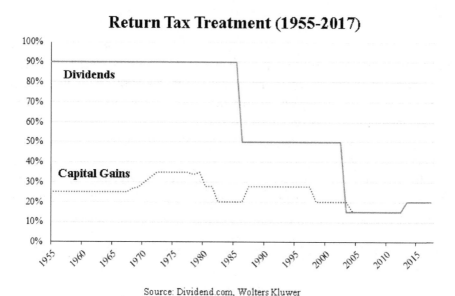

Source: Dividend.com, Wolters Kluwer

Fig. 10.3 Tax Treatment

Volatility and Tax Treatment

Another argument in favor of a yield-focused investment approach stems from the tax advantages of dividend income to investors. While corporations have gained an incentive to distribute earnings, investors have retained the advantage of lower tax rates on dividend income. As of 2018, individuals in the 10% to 15% tax bracket remain exempt from any tax. Those in the middle brackets — 25%, 28%, 33% or 35% — pay 15% at most in capital gains. The highest earners, in the 39.6% bracket, pay 20% in capital gains (plus 3.8% net investment income tax, per the Patient Protection and Affordable Care Act).[46]

On the contrary, all interest income earned from fixed-income securities (other than municipal bond interest) is taxed at the investor's top marginal income tax rate. In many cases, this results in bondholders paying nearly twice as much in taxes on the same income that could be earned in high-yielding stocks.

In addition to lower tax rates on dividend income, investors may also enjoy higher returns that equities can provide over fixed income instruments. In his book, *The Future for Investors*, Jeremy Siegel illustrates that over long-term horizons, stocks have provided just under 7% annualized real, inflation-adjusted return while bonds have yielded only half that.

Though it is true that equity investors receive a "risk premium" over bond investors, dividend-paying companies in the S&P 500 have been shown to provide greater returns than their non-dividend-paying peers with less volatility, as measured by standard deviation. Furthermore, companies committed to growing their dividends have outperformed companies that maintain flat dividends, and have remarkably done so with a smaller standard deviation. Thus, the extolled theory that in order to earn a higher return, one must bear more risk may not hold true when it comes to dividend stocks.

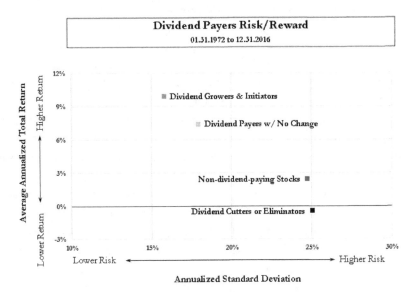

Source: © 2017 Ned Davis Research, Inc. Non-dividend-paying Stocks represents non-dividend-paying stocks of the S&P 500 Index; Dividend Payers w/ No Change represents all dividend-paying stocks of the S&P 500 Index that maintained their existing dividend rate and reflects the reinvestment of all income. The S&P 500 Geometric Equal-Weighted Total Return Index is calculated using monthly equal-weighted geometric averages of the total returns of all dividend-paying stocks and non-dividend-paying stocks.

Fig. 10.4 Dividend Payers Risk/Reward

Early In, Early Out

A client suggested that I had got out of a particular stock too soon because it continued to soar upward after I sold it. We had done well with the stock and I explained the mistake of getting too greedy — the old adage that bulls make money, bears make money, but pigs get slaughtered.

An example of this occurred during the Obama administration when the fear of decreased military spending caused defense stocks like Lockheed and Northrup to take a beating, their P/E ratios ultimately declining to single digits. The dividend ratios on these stocks were around 6%, however, representing what I believed to be a great value so I purchased defense companies when most everyone else was selling them.

It's important to understand that at different times, a company paying dividends can be a value stock, then a blend stock, then a growth stock, at which point I typically sell. As a value investor, I'm usually in early and out early. I get in when sentiment about a stock is negative, and continue to collect the dividend until the P/E ratio elevates to the point where it becomes a blend or even a growth stock. Unlike growth stock investors, part of my reward comes from getting paid by receiving dividends. Growth stock buyers are investing in hope, the hope that the stock goes up. The stocks I buy may go up or go down (as much as growth stocks or more at times), but I keep getting paid while they move in one direction or the other. Momentum investing can keep pushing a stock up until finally, you may be the last guy standing when the music has stopped, and you've got nowhere to sit. Then the stuck plummets and you want to get out...at the same time everyone else is trying to get out. People are losing money and it becomes a race to the door, like a fire.

That's what happened to those defense stocks. But terrorism remained a threat during the duration of the Obama administration and rather quickly, the momentum investors were back in play, scooping up defense stocks, running up the prices. The turnaround generated terrific profits for us in addition to the handsome dividend income we received, but the stocks were no longer cheap. They went from selling at a very cheap multiple to what I believed to be an expensive multiple while the dividend yield was reduced to more than half its original value. I believed it was time to take gains and pay the taxes. Could I have squeezed a little more out of those stocks? Perhaps, but remember the adage: pigs get slaughtered.

Price Down, Dividend Up

High dividend yields and low P/E ratios often go hand in hand. Let's assume a stock selling for $100 and paying a $3 dividend declines to $75. The price has dropped 25% but the dividend yield is now 4%, an increase of 33%. If the stock goes down further, potentially raising the dividend yield even further, I'll buy more shares, providing I believe in the long-term prospects of the company. Many times, a company will raise the dividend to convey confidence in its future prospects. If the firm raises its dividend to $3.25, the stock I bought at 75 now has a dividend yield of 4.3%.

As you can see, higher yields often cause dividend stocks to have a "floor" in that once they get down to a certain price, value and income investors take notice. That's what happened with the defense stocks after they were beaten down: their dividend yields soared. The same thing occurred with healthcare stocks, which had languished through most of the 2000's. When Obamacare was enacted, most investors believed the government was going to take over the healthcare industry, so I was able to take advantage of health care companies selling at very cheap multiples and higher than average dividend yields.

When the price of a sustainable company plunges, it may represent a bargain, just as though the local supermarket announced everything in the store was discounted 25%. But while the supermarket would likely be jammed with bargain hunters, when a stock is on sale, few people get excited.

No Magic Formula

I look for companies that have paid increasing dividends over very long periods of time. There's no mathematical formula or model for identifying these companies.

I want *dividend coverage*, that is, the amount by which a company's earnings exceed its dividends. Typically, I'm looking for at least 50% dividend coverage. The higher a company's earnings are relative to its dividends, the better its dividend coverage and the more flexibility the company has.

A company with good dividend coverage has the option to raise the dividend if it wishes and likewise may still pay the same dividend with little difficulty if earnings decline.[47]

When a company misses its earnings estimate, sometimes by as little as a penny or two, Wall Street often buries it. The analysts go crazy; Jim Cramer is pulling his hair out. The company estimated $6 earnings and announced $5.99.

This is horrible! The stock plummets 10%, then another 10%. The short sellers often get involved, driving it down further. People who own it panic.

But what's changed? They had a bad quarter. They missed by a penny. They missed by .05%. Let's say they missed badly by 25%. Earnings are now down by $1.50, but it still has plenty of money to pay its $3 dividend. All the hand wringing by the talking heads is often much ado about nothing.

I don't understand why so many analysts let their personal opinions so badly cloud their judgement. Though difficult at times, I try to remain agnostic regarding my personal feelings and instead focus on the fundamentals. There are plenty of companies in which I love the product and admire the founder. Elon Musk at Tesla and Jeff Bezos of Amazon come to mind. However, though I may love a product or its leader, I am unwilling to sacrifice my disciplined process by paying too much or investing in companies which fail to align their interests with shareholders by not paying dividends. Straying from this discipline can lead to one being badly harmed when the stock price eventually returns to a reasonable valuation or doesn't meet its astronomical growth expectations.

Don't Chase Yield

An income strategy mistake I continually see made by investors and financial advisors alike is reaching for yield. The worst errors are prevalent among self-directed investors, who don't want the miniscule returns from bank CDs or traditional fixed income vehicles, and don't understand the complexity of the high-yield bond market, so they reach for yield with high-dividend paying stocks or ETFs invested in ostensibly high yielding sectors, such as utilities, real estate, consumer staples, business development corporations (BDCs), or master limited partnerships (MLPs).

The growth of various income strategies over the past five years using ETFs is displayed in graphic 10.5. As you can see, none of the strategies achieved the cumulative return level of the Altrius Disciplined Alpha Income strategy or broad based value indices. Though I've often invested in these sectors due to their generally lower volatility and higher yields, I'm glad I've avoided them over the past five years as their valuations were driven higher by investors reaching for yield. As such, I rightly believed their total return potential was limited over a longer period of time.

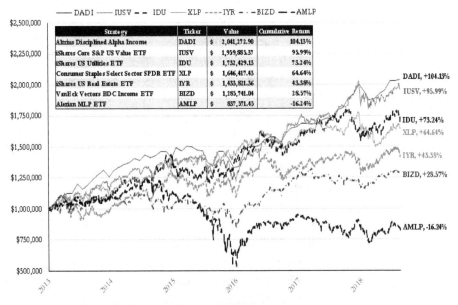

Altrius Global Income Growth of $1,000,000* vs. Income Strategies

Strategy	Ticker	Value	Cumulative Return
Altrius Disciplined Alpha Income	DADI	$ 2,041,272.90	104.13%
iShares Core S&P US Value ETF	IUSV	$ 1,959,985.37	95.99%
iShares US Utilities ETF	IDU	$ 1,732,429.13	73.24%
Consumer Staples Select Sector SPDR ETF	XLP	$ 1,646,417.43	64.64%
iShares US Real Estate ETF	IYR	$ 1,433,821.36	43.38%
VanEck Vectors BDC Income ETF	BIZD	$ 1,285,741.04	28.57%
Alerian MLP ETF	AMLP	$ 837,371.45	-16.24%

*Portfolio Growth of $1,000,000 assumes reinvestment of all dividends since inception.
Time period represented is 2/12/2013-9/30/2018. All data represented is gross of fees.

Fig. 10.5 ETF Income Strategies

Utilities

Cumulative return: 73.24%

Utilities are a popular choice for investors chasing yield. When interest rates are low, they willingly pay high prices thereby bidding multiples higher and yields much lower than their historic valuations. When this occurs, there's little cushion for many utilities. If energy prices rise, they're largely unable to pass on the additional cost to consumers because of political restrictions. If the price of the coal or natural gas they need to make electricity goes higher, the company's earnings are compressed and its growth potential — even its dividend — may not be sustainable.

Investors (and many advisors) tend to overlook a company's earnings and valuation when chasing yield, which can be a critical factor in its ability to continue paying its dividend. When a company is earning less than it needs to cover its dividend, there's a possibility the dividend may be cut.

Business Development Companies

Cumulative return: 28.57%

A business development company (BDC) makes investments in developing companies and in firms that are financially distressed. A major difference between BDCs and venture capital funds is that BDCs allow smaller, non-accredited investors to invest in startup companies.[48]

BDCs are known for their enticing high yields, which can be an irresistible lure for retirees. One egregious example of how investors reaching for yield with BDCs can get badly hurt financially is Triangle Capital Corp (TCAP) with its headquarters close to our Raleigh/Durham office. TCAP made some poor investments in the companies it was lending money to and, over a 12-month period, suffered losses of approximately 40% before being forced into bankruptcy. Virtually the entire investment portfolio was liquidated through a sale to BSP Asset Acquisition (BSP) in 2018. The firm's executives will fare far better than its investors, receiving $17 million in golden parachute money.

I have generally avoided BDCs for numerous reasons and specifically did so during this trailing five-year period as investors were lured to their higher yields. BDCs' investments in distressed and small to mid-sized companies during their initial stages of development can be riskier by its nature. In addition, BDCs' use of leverage in these smaller companies, which tend to be illiquid and have subjective fair value estimates, can further exacerbate its risk. During a recession, or even in sound economic times, BDCs can fail to generate the earnings necessary to pay the high yields investors find so alluring and, at worst, suffer catastrophic decay as was the case for Triangle Capital Corporation.

Master Limited Partnerships

Cumulative return: negative -16.24%

Master Limited Partnerships are primarily involved with the energy arena–pipelines, crude oil storage, refined product storage, exploration and production of oil or gas — but may be involved in diverse areas such as Cemeteries, Investment Firms, Amusement Parks and Sand Mining.[49]

Individual investors love MLPs, once again lured by the attractive yields. As you can tell by the sector's miserable 5-year negative returns, the advertised distributions have been largely unsustainable as their earnings have been hammered.

Over the last five years, I've had zero allocation to MLPs, BDCs, and REITs. Investors starved for income gravitate to them like moths attracted to light. They reach for yield, and just as moths are evaporated, so too are investor portfolios when valuations aren't considered.

The Next Hot Thing

As previously mentioned, mutual fund companies are brilliant marketers when it comes to providing whatever the investing public perceives as a hot issue. One of the more recent examples of this ploy is the emergence of the so-called low beta ETFs.

When the mutual fund complex sensed that financial advisors and investors were looking for lower volatility in the post financial crisis world, it invented a new asset class — low beta ETFs — and dispatched its wholesalers out to the financial advisory community, who eagerly gobbled up the new products and stampeded their clients into these formulaic passive strategies. One example is the Invesco SPLV, purported to be a low volatility ETF offering a "smoother ride and better risk/reward profile than the S&P 500," according to Morningstar analysis.

Drilling down into SPLV reveals that nearly 50% of the fund consists of just three sectors: utilities (19%), real estate (15%), and consumer defensive (15%). Performance ramped up during 2014 and 2015 as this type of investment caught fire with investors jumping on the bandwagon, driving the price higher. Then, after two years of great performance, it took a precipitous plunge from the first percentile in its Morningstar Large Blend category to the 90th percentile in 2016, temporarily bouncing back to a mediocre 38th in 2017, only to drop once again to 75th as of this writing in 2018.

It's the same story retold over and over again. A financial crisis and extended period of low interest rates is followed by the investing public's outcry for something with low volatility and high dividends. The mutual fund industry responds with products that address that wish and the bull rush is on. It works for a while as investors continue to pile in and bid up the price, not unlike momentum stocks, which do well until everyone starts talking about them and gets on board. Then, as more and more investors pile in, they grow in value and get too expensive, eventually resulting in a lower return.

As money continues to flow into these funds, it has to be put to work, often into the same overvalued stocks based upon the ETFs formula. Bear in mind, however, that the top performance is often not due to stock selection as much as it may be due to the continued onrush of new investors coming in, pushing up the asset prices of the underlying stocks and ETFs. Pity the poor investors who are the last ones in.

The mistake many investors make is screening exclusively for companies paying the highest dividend yield, resulting in their portfolios becoming loaded up on just a few sectors like utilities, consumer staples and real estate. That does not provide adequate diversification.

During the last five years, I'm happy to say I resisted the urge to chase yield (as I always have) and stayed out of all these sectors. Dividends are an important component to total return, but must not be chased to the exclusion of a consideration of valuation.

Disciplined Process

As an investment manager, I have steadfastly refused to buy stocks my analysis considers to be overpriced. An example of this is Starbucks, the trendy coffee chain with locations in seemingly every city and town across the U.S.

Though Starbucks is the coffee shop of choice for some of us at Altrius, I believe that investing in a company simply because it makes products one likes can trap investors into overpaying for its shares and, until recently, thought the company expensive. Previously trading at over 30 times trailing earnings (more than twice that of our Disciplined Alpha Dividend strategy) with a dividend yield of around 1.5% (less than half that of our Disciplined Alpha Dividend strategy) — Starbucks remained outside of our value discipline in past years. However, the company caught my attention after a recent selloff and I added it to our portfolios in early August, 2018.

Though it's headquartered in Seattle, I wouldn't label Starbucks an American company. While 68% of its revenues were generated in the Americas over the trailing twelve-month period ending in June, this figure is down from 74% over the same period five years ago, but not for lack of domestic revenue growth, which has continued at 9% annually. Instead, Starbucks has been rapidly expanding into overseas markets, particularly China and Asia Pacific (CAP), which has seen annualized revenue growth of 37% over the past five years and is approaching one-fifth of the company's total revenues. In China alone, the number of company-operated stores has tripled during this time period, versus only 3% annual store growth in the Americas.

The CAP segment is largely driven by China, where the middle class is expected to double to 600 million by 2022 and will drive coffee consumption in the region. To capitalize on this growth opportunity, the company has unveiled plans to double its store count in China to over 6,000 by 2022, opening a new store every 15 hours as it expands into 100 new cities with a combined population nearly 100 times greater than that of Los Angeles.

As a result of this growth strategy in China, Starbucks' operations in the region may conceivably overtake the scale of its business in its home market within the coming decade.

While I screen for companies with histories of steady dividend payments, more important to our clients are future dividend growth prospects in order to provide income through the market's cyclical perturbations. Starbucks has such potential, having paid a dividend each quarter since early 2010 and grown its payout by 27.5% per year. Additionally, the company recently announced a 20% dividend hike that took effect in the third quarter of 2018.

Though its yield has remained below the 2% level for most of the past eight years, Starbucks recently eclipsed this threshold after its sharp price drop and its yield sat just below 2.8% when I added the stock to our portfolios.

Over the past four years, Starbucks has traded at a P/E ratio of around 30, well above our Global Income strategy's average of 14, suggesting that investors have been willing to pay a high premium for the company's shares. However, following its 15% selloff at the end of June, we purchased Starbucks at 16 times trailing earnings, a multiple we view as an attractive discount to the company's fundamental value.

Investing is more art than science and one cannot utilize a formula to guarantee investment success, although plenty of people will try to sell you such a system. Every investment entails risk, but I believe that investing in companies with global revenue growth potential, steady dividend histories, and attractive valuations better enables me to manage this risk and has been the primary reason for Altrius' success over the past two plus decades.

Value of Consistent Dividend Income

Any experienced investment analyst knows the importance of trying to see through the huge amounts of data, reports, and commentary published on a company to get to the core of what is happening at the transaction level and try to determine the handful of critical issues concerning its competitive value proposition. Peter Lynch made famous the approach of becoming familiar with a company's story by simply visiting its stores and using its products. A number of successful investors spend more of their time on the phone and meeting with company management than digging through 10-Ks.

Similarly, the money management industry can also be over-complicated and distorted by the seemingly infinite number of ways of analyzing and tracking investments. Many fund managers who make the ultimate decisions regarding which companies to allocate capital to are disconnected from their investors by multiple layers of due diligence and research through funds of funds, consultants, open architecture platforms, approval committees, distribution and client service employees, and a variety of other structures. These fund managers may under-appreciate the psychological and informational benefit that consistent income provides to a portfolio and its investor. Even in a down market, stocks that generate consistent cash flows ' can provide peace of mind to investors, particularly those who are subject to behavioral biases such as loss aversion, anchoring, myopia, and others that make investing an emotional endeavor.

In light of the role that dividends play in aligning interests in our increasingly complex and interconnected world, the ongoing demographic shift towards a preference for income as opposed to gains on capital, and changing perceptions of value post financial crisis, it seems prudent to reevaluate firms' dividend policies and the emphasis that fund managers place on those policies when making investment decisions.

> *"Basically, price fluctuations have only one significant meaning for the true investor. They provide him with an opportunity to buy wisely when prices fall sharply and to sell wisely when they advance a great deal. At other times, he will do better if he forgets about the stock market and pays attention to his dividend returns and to the operating results of his companies."*
> Benjamin Graham

CHAPTER ELEVEN

Smart Beta

Keep Your Ears Up To Mind the Risks

According to Investopedia, "The goal of smart beta is to obtain alpha, lower risk or increase diversification...(seeking) the best construction of an optimally diversified portfolio. In effect, smart beta is a combination of efficient-market hypothesis and value investing."

Long before the term was hijacked into a marketing ploy by financial companies, my risk management investment process employed some of these characteristics. However, my definition of smart beta differs and employs an active management process characterized by three aspects of portfolio management which I believe may lead to potentially superior risk-adjusted returns.

> ➢ Portfolio management and security selection is based on three factors: global macro outlook, value, and income — which I believe are crucial in generating total return. Rather than following an index, construction and selection are based upon the fundamentals and a tactical allocation is employed to flexibly position our portfolios to capitalize on opportunities.
> ➢ Our portfolio holdings are *weighted equally* in order to diversify adequately and prevent a small number of securities from driving portfolio performance.
> ➢ A process of contrarian rebalancing on a conditional basis helps bring holdings back to equal weights and manage risk.

> When deemed necessary, our firm trims positions that have grown in value and uses the proceeds to purchase those which have declined in value, which I believe retain earnings growth potential.

Though counter intuitive, trimming or selling the outperformers and buying underperformers are exactly what I believe disciplined investors should do. Most importantly, I feel strongly that this action is critical from a risk management perspective. A structured risk management strategy is essential throughout the security selection, monitoring, and sell decision process. There is no such thing as a formula or procedure which can guarantee mistakes will not be made. However, by maintaining a data-driven, facts-oriented investment management process, one can better avoid the biases that can often lead to poor risk management decisions.

As an added risk management component to the investment process, we create worst case and best case scenarios for evaluating market opportunities and risk. There's no hesitation to sell securities that I believe are at risk based on fundamental factors. By remaining agile and focused on our portfolio holdings at all times, I'm prepared to sell securities that are not performing fundamentally or for which I have identified better candidates to maximize portfolio return and to potentially minimize portfolio risk.

That said, one can never avoid price declines as selloffs can occur based upon multiple exogenous events outside the control of a company or simply due to a market decline or recession. Though the mathematicians and economic models which drive current day algorithms garner the most attention and weight for today's financial portfolio management teams, I feel that risk should not be measured in terms of standard deviation or beta — though such measures provide some useful guidance. Instead, I believe risk should be based primarily on the intrinsic value of a company, based upon its cash flow, dividend, and potential earnings growth.

This is in opposition to what you regularly hear on the financial networks, where the mantra is "the trend is your friend." A recent example was Jim Cramer telling viewers he continues to buy the momentum stocks that persist in rising. Interestingly, he also mentioned how portfolio managers suffer when stocks are declining because of redemptions. As a contrarian, value investor, I thought to myself, he has it exactly reversed: you should be buying the stocks that are going down rather than purchasing overpriced momentum stocks.

I understand his perspective that hedge fund, mutual fund, and investment managers get overrun with redemptions when stocks go down and their performance sinks; that's when clients clamor to get out. On the other hand, our clients get paid to wait because of our focus on dividends and income. They understand the concept of buying something that's going down in value. That's the idea behind my risk management philosophy. It's an overall portfolio management process that includes everything from a global macro outlook, to a value discipline, to reliance on immediate income to mitigate risk, patiently waiting for a company to achieve full value while its stock price or the market is in decline. It's diligent selection and disciplined, equal weighting rebalancing. It's the exact opposite of what Cramer and most traders on television tell you to do.

They typify the Wall Street mindset: Don't fight the tape; buy the winners and sell the losers; the trend is your friend. Constantly chasing momentum.

But most investors jump on the wagon too late and, when the trend eventually changes because the momentum stocks have become so heavily overvalued, they get creamed, having paid too dearly for the companies.

On one of the financial channels dedicated to such momentum trading principles, they were talking about Campbell's versus Grubhub and why the latter is a better choice. It reminded me of a blog I wrote about Shake Shack versus McDonalds. The fast traders all would have chosen Shake Shack over boring old McDonald's and they all would have been wrong. Though we didn't own either company, I found myself yelling at the TV, "It's Campbell's, not Grubhub you muttonheads." They made assertions that Grubhub would continue to grow at 20+% indefinitely. Momentum chasing investors—along with market technicians I equate with astrologists—prefer to own the GrubHub's of the market, not boring, lackluster companies like Campbell's.

At the time, Grubhub was selling at 100 times earnings, 60 times forward earnings, and not paying a dividend. Why would you own that? Is it possible the Grubhub believers will be right five years from now? Perhaps. Maybe Grubhub will become the greatest company since Google, but I don't think so and certainly don't believe the risk/reward tradeoff a prudent investment.

In contrast, why not consider an investment in a beaten down company like Campbell's which was selling at 14 times earnings and paying a 3.5% dividend? Certainly, it is a more prudent investment. Though many money managers and financial advisors promise astronomical returns and take extraordinary risk in attempting to achieve such promises, I simply attempt to get our clients to—and through—retirement.

As I've mentioned in earlier chapters, I've seen too many highly intelligent individuals, and too many self-directed investors, blow up their portfolios, hedge funds, mutual funds, and businesses by trying to keep up with such momentum. Instead, I'm perfectly content to hit singles and provide sound risk adjusted returns rather than swing for the fences. That's what smart beta means to me. It's focusing on macroeconomic conditions, value, income, global growth potential; equally weighting our positions and contrarian rebalancing.

Campbell's may have negatives, particularly in the short-term—a lot of short interest and mathematical algorithms pushing it lower—but I don't want to own Campbell's for a day or a week or a month. I want to own it over the next five to ten years. Should I decide to invest in a company like Campbell's, my clients would patiently collect the 3.5% dividend, which is their salary, while we wait for the company to turn around and reach full value...unlike the investment managers chasing momentum.

My clients pay me to think. I believe smart beta should be smart. It should be thoughtful, from both an investment and a tax perspective. Despite use by some ETFs trying to embellish their appeal, there are no magical mathematical algorithms. Many times, after a stock has run up and I think it's still really cheap, I don't want some formulaic algorithm to restrict me from leaving the weighting at 1.2% instead of 1%. There are times when I might not want clients to pay taxes on it. On the other hand, if a stock has run up and is starting to look expensive, I will rebalance or sell the company. Conditional rebalancing is part of our investment policy.

Risk Management

Academics and portfolio managers often refer to standard deviation and beta when measuring risk. A beta greater than 1 signifies that a portfolio is theoretically more volatile than a particular index. The higher the standard deviation, the greater the volatility it displays from a particular mean. Using the average annual standard deviation to measure risk can be useful, but like beta, can be an imperfect measure. Mathematically, it can certainly lull one into complacency during less volatile periods. More importantly, neither measure adequately identifies the true risk of a company—or more succinctly, the potential for loss.

Standard deviation is simply volatility: however, in my opinion, risk shouldn't be identified merely as how volatile something is in relation to a hypothetical baseline. Risk is not something that can be easily or conveniently measured. It's more art than science and establishing a security's value calls for extensive experience and judgment.

Regarding standard deviation, as previously noted in chapter 9 (graphic 9.1), over the past 60 years, the average annual return of the highest P/E stocks badly lagged that of the lowest P/E stocks (7.86% vs 12.92%) while simultaneously displaying 16% higher standard deviation. Investors buying high P/E growth stocks received the poorest returns while suffering the highest volatility. On the other hand, the lowest P/E stocks delivered the best returns with near-lowest volatility. If you're willing to buy the stuff that everyone hates — the lowest P/E stocks — and they eventually outperform, it becomes a "have your cake and eat it too" story.

It takes a strong stomach to be a value investor buying low P/E stocks, especially during the past eight years, when many traders, pundits, and advisors are telling you to put all your money into the big momentum stocks like Facebook and Amazon and declaring value investing dead. They insist it makes no sense to buy stocks everyone hates because they just keep going lower. The majority of investors are enthralled with a handful of momentum stocks and so the focus of the media (and the financial community) has remained with growth stocks. Tune into a financial news show and the FANG stocks are sure to dominate their coverage. These few stocks have helped drive the passive index funds, a potentially precarious situation at such lofty valuations and earnings expectations.

In 2006, I had dinner with Jeremy Siegel, Professor of Finance at the Wharton School of the University of Pennsylvania and one of the financial industry's most highly regarded economists, a man whose research on dividends has had a significant influence on me. We were joined by Brian Gendreau, who was a senior economist with ING Investments at the time. While discussing portfolio management, I asked Gendreau if he thought real estate was overvalued. He said "yes." I then asked him what ING's current allocation to real estate was and he said it was 4.3%. I responded cynically, "You're telling me that you believe REITs are overvalued, so why isn't your allocation to real estate 4.1% or 3.9%? Why not a zero allocation? Our clients are paying us to think." He knew I was busting his chops, but the logic behind ING's REIT allocation for their balanced portfolios—along with every other investment management firm and bank—seemed imprudent to me.

This goes straight to the Wall Street mentality regarding efficient market asset allocation, in this case, regarding real estate prior to 2008. Economists and managers, adhering to the efficient market frontier, believed their portfolios should always include a real estate allocation.

Early in my career, I reasoned that the efficient market hypothesis and modern portfolio theory espousing the construction of a broad array of assets along an efficient frontier to optimize a portfolio was a flawed theory. Some sectors, such as emerging markets, were just too volatile, and I avoided them because the risk reward equation didn't make sense. To me, the best way to manage risk is not through an allocation to every asset class along an efficient frontier. Again, clients pay me to think. If I believe emerging markets, real estate or a particular company is overvalued, the allocation should be zero. I'm not going to worry about trailing some arbitrary index, or that I might be beaten by another advisor or money manager who has their money invested in REITs because the sector is temporarily flying high.

Today, many money managers and advisors are afraid of missing out on FANG stocks, just as many were afraid of missing the dot com frenzy. They're afraid to look foolish or lose clients. I'm not afraid to look foolish. I'll sit here and try my best to get my clients and investors a prudent rate of return which, for some people, is boring. So many investors believe there is some secret formula that's going to continually get them great returns. Those investors won't hire me because I'm not part of the herd chasing momentum; I'm just looking to get my clients—people who've made a lot of money and don't want to lose it—a prudent rate of return, and help them avoid making dumb mistakes by taking imprudent risks with their portfolio.

I'm not saying that people who believe in momentum investing are wrong. Over the past seven years, it's been the best place to invest. The problem is when it goes wrong, when it turns, it turns hard. As a value investor during a period like the last eight years, you can look foolish for a long time. Value is being called dead. When I start hearing that kind of commentary, I realize we're likely closer to the end of this cycle.

Many investors have no idea how their portfolios would fare if the equity market took a big hit, according to a risk-tolerance survey by FinMason. Most investors are unaware of the amount of risk in their equity portfolios. As a result, these investors make poor, costly sell decisions at the worst time: when the markets do correct.[50]

In addition to being cognizant of managing market and security risk, we continually attempt to gauge the personal risk tolerance of our clients. For a client investing a million dollars with our firm, I understand it is your hard-earned money painstakingly saved over a lifetime and potentially your entire life's savings. If you are near or in retirement, I also recognize that you need income to fund your retirement as you can't retire putting your money in the bank at 1%. You need to take some risk to achieve your goals and your greatest risk may be taking none at all as inflation and taxes erode your purchasing power.

As the chief investment strategist of the firm, managing risk from both a portfolio and individual security level is an ongoing process. I'm continually evaluating risk and reward on multiple levels and repeatedly questioning where I might be wrong. I understand that I cannot control the economic and market winds which continually shift. What I do have some control over are the dividends and interest that can provide substantial income for retirement needs, better enabling my clients to withstand eventual and unavoidable market corrections and volatility. My objective for a balanced portfolio of bonds and stocks is to have its one million produce income of $45 to $50k a year.

People really don't know what their true risk tolerance is until something happens to test it. Under most circumstances, when an investor's portfolio goes down from $1 million to $800k, they panic and liquidate their positions. With my income based investment process, our clients continue to be paid $45k to $50k annually even after such a 20% decline—as long as Pepsi and the other companies in which we are invested continue to pay their dividends and interest. I understand that this strategy can be boring, but it is this beautifully boring strategy that has enabled our clients to withstand several severe market corrections over the past two plus decades. Past performance is never a guarantee of future returns; however, I believe this strategy is highly effective and the key to the fact that none of our clients ever had to go back to work.

CHAPTER TWELVE

Global Asset Allocation

Tirelessly searching for opportunities

While value and dividends form an integral part of a three-pronged strategy, setting the asset allocation appropriately for each client is regularly the most consequential aspect of the process and critical to achieving a sound risk-adjusted return.

Though there is great debate among money managers as to whether a top-down, "big picture" economic approach or bottom-up, fundamental analysis of companies is more effective, I've always believed this a silly argument because to me, both are essential to good portfolio management. Though it may be difficult to read the tea leaves of various economic factors, in aggregate, they often give hints of where one should tilt a portfolio in relation to stocks or bonds.

I am not suggesting that anyone can predict the business cycle or a recession. However, it is possible to discern how a top-down, broader view of the economy can drive market cycles, market segments, and ultimately, individual security prices. From that perspective, one must also look at the world globally rather than from the simple prism of their geography. Too many investors have a home bias and don't look outside their country of origin for opportunities.

A global macro perspective drives my investment analysis because I believe global revenue generation is a key component to growth and sustainability. I look to invest in companies with global growth opportunities. While aware of the risks of a global economy, I'm unafraid to take contrarian positions.

Economic Scenario Analysis

In order to appropriately set an asset allocation strategy, I analyze the economic climate and craft best case, worst case, and base case (expected) scenarios. This analysis is a key component of my global macro, top-down approach. As an economist, I always look at things from the top-down first, then the bottom-up. The allocation is a critical first step.

At Altrius, we believe that global asset allocation valuations matter. Predicated on this belief, we maintain a series of three economic scenarios under which the economy may fall at any one time. By analyzing the valuations inherent in the current economic scenario, we believe we are better positioned to identify securities at the sector, industry and individual company level that are best positioned to add significant value to our portfolio over time.

ECONOMIC SCENARIOS *Our likely scenario*			
	Bear	Base	Bull
S&P 500 at 2641, Barclays Aggregate yield at 3.1%, MSCI Europe Index at 1751, BofA ML High Yield Cash Pay Index at 6.3%.			
Equities	Estimate	Estimate	Estimate
U.S. Equities	-8.1%	3.7%	8.5%
Developed Int'l – Europe	-8.1%	8.4%	14.4%
REITs	-3.8%	2.7%	5.1%
Fixed Income			
Investment-Grade Bonds	3.4%	2.1%	0.9%
High-Yield Bonds	1.6%	4.8%	5.3%
TIPS	2.2%	1.3%	-1.1%

Source: Altrius Capital

Fig. 12.1 Economic Scenarios

That's not to say any economic analysis—mine or any other analyst's—is spot on. These things can be inexact. I look at the bear and bull estimates and ask, what if one of them is right? The bears and bulls tend to consistently be the same people, like perpetual doomsayer Nouriel Roubini, an economist known as "Dr. Doom" for his dark predictions. Robert Shiller, professor of economics at Yale, leans bearish, although not all in like Roubini. On the other hand, Jeremy Siegel, professor of finance at Wharton School, is an enduring bull who almost always believes the stock market is headed up. These are exceptionally intelligent people but they're human.

I believe that after modeling for what the bear economist thinks is going to happen and what the bull economist thinks, the truth is usually somewhere in between.

Global Consumption Trends

When you hear economists say "global macro," what they're talking about is the macroeconomic environment. Demographic trends and geographic demand serve to drive global economic growth. The potential for consumption among major countries is an important factor is assessing investment potential in various industry sectors.

For example, roughly 17.5 million light vehicles were sold in the U.S. during 2016, an increase of less than a half percent over the record set in 2015.[51] Worldwide, 77 million cars were sold, which means there were 60 million vehicles sold in countries outside the U.S. during 2016.[52]

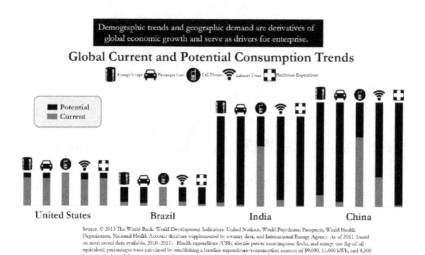

Fig. 12.2 Global Consumption

As illustrated in Graphic 12.2, while sales of cars in the U.S. far exceeds those of China and India, the potential for sales growth in those two countries is enormously greater. One reason is that 95% of American households already own a car.[53] Conversely, only about 25% of Chinese households own a car. The potential for growth is obviously much greater in China, as it is in India, Brazil, and other countries. The potential for Ford and GM to sell cars in China is gigantic. As of 2016, China is now GM's largest market. Strong sales in China more than made up for slower sales in the United States. GM recorded its fourth straight year of record sales even as U.S. sales fell slightly, the first decline in GM's home market since 2009.[54]

Looking at the graphic, one asks, where is there opportunity to sell more oil, cars or cell phones? Thinking of companies from a global perspective instead of a myopic home bias can open ideas for opportunities.

In America, virtually everyone drives; everyone has a cell phone. The potential for global growth in cars, cell phones, energy usage, internet users, and healthcare expenditures dwarfs that of the U.S. market. That's why the global macro component and thinking globally is so important. People get aroused because of political changes, such as a change in our immigration policy, but what impact does that have on how many cars are purchased in China? None. Granted, policies like import tariffs can have an impact when they trigger trade wars. If we put a tariff on imported steel and the Chinese respond by imposing a 25% tariff on American automobiles, few Chinese will buy an American car. That's an argument for diversification. Owning Japanese, German and Korean auto manufacturers can help cushion the impact of such a contingency.

I avoid investing in companies that have saturated their markets, such as retail outlets that have locations in virtually every small town in America. There's nowhere for these companies to go unless they are capable of expanding overseas. There exists tremendous growth potential outside the U.S. For example, in China where increasing numbers of that population come into the cities and the middle class. Companies that are able to successfully penetrate overseas markets can continue to grow their revenues and earnings.

I believe the best thing for us to do is maintain our global macro value approach, realizing that people around the globe will continue to drink Starbucks coffee, eat Frito-Lay chips (a subsidiary of Pepsi), and buy tech products that use Intel chips.

Corporate Headquarters Are Irrelevant

People regularly confuse what constitutes an American or an international company. The distinction can be made difficult by where a company is headquartered. Back in the 1970's and 1980's, it was much clearer: U.S. stocks were U.S. and international stocks were international. The world has changed and is now global. Nestle is selling chocolate in America. Hershey's is selling chocolate in Europe. Where a company is headquartered doesn't matter. Though taxes and currency have an impact on earnings, where a company's revenue is generated is the principal driver.

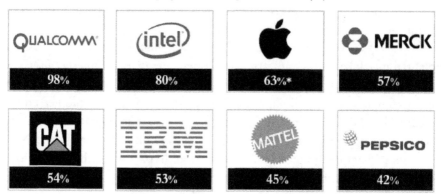

A Sampling of Major US Brands with Foreign Revenues Above 40% of Total Revenues

Are domestic companies really domestic anymore? While a company may be headquartered in the United States, investing requires understanding the drivers of a company's bottom line.

Sources: Data represented is as of company's latest 10-K filing for the period ending 12.31.2017 (*Fiscal year end as of 9.30.2017 for Qualcomm Inc. & Apple Inc). Foreign Revenue is based on Total Revenue – Domestic Revenue. Logos are trademarks of their respective owners and are used for illustrative purposes and should not be construed as an endorsement or sponsorship of Altrias.

Fig.12.3 Foreign Revenues

Graphic 12.3 is an example of how many companies perceived as American actually receive a substantial portion of their revenues from outside the U.S.

Intel is not an American company because 80% of its revenues comes from overseas. Apple is not an American company; the majority of its revenue is generated from overseas. Caterpillar isn't an American company; it just happens to be headquartered in Peoria, Illinois. If America taxes it too much, it can leave, and likely will. Eaton Corp was an Ohio company but felt America was taxing it too much and so moved overseas. Transocean was a Texas company but moved its headquarters to Switzerland for the same reason. Both companies derived most of their revenues from overseas but were viewed by many as American companies.

To me, it's silly to call Intel or Qualcomm a U.S. company. Over 90% of Qualcomm's revenue is generated from outside the U.S. For Apple, it's over 60%. Should conditions, taxes or economics dictate, there's not much to prevent

Apple from moving to another country. On the other hand, Switzerland-headquartered Nestle garners 98% of its revenues from outside of Switzerland.

Investors often have a home bias, but investing should be viewed with a global perspective. Europe, for example, is starting to rebound and European assets are becoming attractive relative to the U.S. A similar thing is occurring with growth and value stocks. The momentum stocks of the world have had a major run that feels like an eternity. As a value investor, I'm sometimes asked why not simply put everything into the S&P 500? Well, the S&P has a less than 2% dividend yield and its high valuation is driven by growth stocks with large market capitalizations. Investors have to hope those stocks keep going up in order to sell shares to get the income they need. Investors riding the momentum express have to hope nothing happens to derail it. They are investing in hope. I'm not investing in hope. I'm thinking globally, looking for stocks at attractive valuations that provide the dividend yield my clients need to drive total return and steady income. Whether those stocks are domiciled within or outside the U.S. is irrelevant.

Investors who lack a global perspective assume everything outside of the U.S. is a single homogenous market, whereas it's actually an amalgam of big cities, small towns, villages, and agricultural areas. It's a puzzle with a million pieces, not a huge solitary monolith.

I believe many investors make the mistake of looking at McDonald's as an American company and Nestle as an international company. When setting an allocation, I turn that perspective on its head and look at them from a global macro viewpoint. Where their revenue is generated is much more important than where they are headquartered. To me, McDonald's is a global company, not an American company, because more than 70% of its revenues comes from overseas. It's a global investment with the ability to grow overseas.

Global Growth Revenues

Again, setting the allocation, industries, and sectors by correctly identifying the global macro conditions and the cycle we are in from a top-down approach is the first part of the process. Then, conversely, a bottom-up approach is used to pinpoint the right individual securities in which to invest.

This may sound a bit counterintuitive, because I'm an advocate of not trying to predict the market. No one can consistently predict whether the market is headed up or down. What I try to do is determine where growth is likely to come from globally, irrespective of where a company is headquartered.

You may have seen the Callan periodic chart (graphic 12.4) that depicts how the performance of various sectors rise and fall each year.

The Callan Periodic Table of Investment Returns

Annual Returns for Key Indices Ranked in Order of Performance (1998–2017)

The Callan Periodic Table of Investment Returns conveys the strong *case for diversification* across asset classes (stocks vs. bonds), investment styles (growth vs. value), capitalizations (large vs. small), and equity markets (U.S. vs. non-U.S.). The Table highlights the uncertainty inherent in all capital markets. Rankings change every year. Also noteworthy is the difference between absolute and relative performance, as returns for the top-performing asset class span a wide range over the past 20 years.

Callan | Knowledge. Experience. Integrity.

© 2018 Callan LLC

A printable copy of *The Callan Periodic Table of Investment Returns* is available on our website at www.callan.com

Fig. 12.4 Callan Chart

Last year, Emerging Markets was the top performer, after being middle of the pack the year before and at the very bottom three of the five years before that. Not only do sectors yoyo from year to year, they sometimes continue a cycle for several years, as did Emerging Markets from 2003 through 2007, when it outperformed for five consecutive years before plummeting to the bottom in 2008, only to return to the top spot in 2009. What a roller coaster ride that provided for investors.

I think the Callan chart may have been useful back in the 1970's and 1980's when it was easier to identify if companies were U.S. or international. Now that the lines have blurred, it's difficult to say whether a company is one or the other because they are selling globally. Today, it's far more important to determine *from where the revenues are generated*, and where the global growth is occurring.

Where is the greatest demographic potential? Where is demand growing and slowing? What sectors are overvalued and undervalued? Within these sectors, which stocks are the cheapest? Which have the lower P/E's? Which are paying above average dividends and growing? These considerations from both a top-down and bottom-up analysis are critical to making sound investment decisions.

Even Buffett Can Get It Wrong

During his annual shareholder meeting in 2018, Warren Buffett advised investors to put all their money into the Vanguard 500 index. I disagree with his advice for two reasons.

First, putting all your money into an ETF or mutual fund which invests in the S&P 500 index provides limited international diversification. Second, indexes such as the S&P 500 are market cap weighted and heavily biased towards growth. An example is the SPDR® S&P 500 ETF (SPY).

SPDR® S&P 500 ETF (SPY)

Holdings	% Portfolio Weight	Shares Owned
Apple Inc	4.13	50,769,269
Microsoft Corp	3.53	84,846,035
Amazon.com Inc	2.96	4,533,073
Berkshire Hathaway Inc B	1.75	21,569,836
Johnson & Johnson	1.64	29,683,669
JPMorgan Chase & Co	1.58	37,186,707
Facebook Inc A	1.57	26,684,390
Exxon Mobil Corp	1.50	46,845,540
Alphabet Inc Class C	1.41	3,406,681
Alphabet Inc A	1.39	3,307,490

Fig. 12.5 SPDR® S&P 500 ETF

This is a broad market index similar to the Russell 1000/3000 or Wilshire 5000 which contains more companies but is still market weighted. At the time of this writing, a massive 20+% of the SPY's assets are in the top 10 holdings.

Another popular ETF, iShares Russell 1000 Growth, is heavily weighted in momentum stocks with over 30% of its assets in its top 10 holdings.

iShares Russell 1000 Growth ETF (IWF)

Holdings	% Portfolio Weight	Shares Owned
Apple Inc	8.28	15,340,667
Microsoft Corp	5.70	22,128,780
Amazon.com Inc	5.19	1,282,942
Facebook Inc A	2.85	7,729,342
Alphabet Inc A	2.44	923,765
Alphabet Inc Class C	2.42	929,978
Visa Inc Class A	2.00	5,841,267
UnitedHealth Group Inc	1.95	3,072,217
The Home Depot Inc	1.62	3,704,627
Boeing Co	1.54	1,747,885

Fig. 12.6 iShares Russell 1000 ETF

The Invesco QQQ Trust (based on the NASDAQ index) has a whopping 55+% of its assets in its top ten holdings.

Invesco QQQ Trust (QQQ)

Holdings	% Portfolio Weight	Shares Owned
Apple Inc	13.20	40,306,591
Amazon.com Inc	9.99	4,070,309
Microsoft Corp	9.99	63,992,723
Alphabet Inc Class C	4.60	2,919,754
Facebook Inc A	4.50	20,125,892
Alphabet Inc A	3.99	2,494,422
Intel Corp	2.73	38,479,428
Cisco Systems Inc	2.64	39,246,394
Comcast Corp Class A	2.13	38,158,292
PepsiCo Inc	1.94	11,802,742
Netflix Inc	1.70	3,633,956

Fig.12.7 PowerShares QQQ

I have another issue with Buffett's suggestion: most investors do not have the wherewithal nor the temperament to stomach downward spirals like the 40+% declines that have occurred twice during the past two decades. The NASDAQ suffered a collapse that saw it drop much further during the tech bubble. When investors experienced such a decline during the financial crisis, they fled the market in huge numbers and went to cash, missing out on much of the subsequent upturn. Imagine someone retiring just as that decline began, seeing their $1 million portfolio cut in half.

Market cap indexes with heavily concentrated holdings, such as the S&P 500, are prime candidates for these types of principal losses. Buffett's home bias ("Don't bet against America" he has frequently said) may be a patriotic posture, but is he sure the U.S. is going to continue to be dominant? Can investors afford to ignore the enormous potential of markets like China, India, Brazil, and others? I have risked my life for this country but as an investor, I think it's a mistake to say "USA, USA" and discount the rest of the world.

I like Nestle better than Hershey. Nestle is a wonderful company that's growing globally and just happens to be headquartered overseas. Budweiser is an example of a great American brand that was inefficient and was taken over by InBev, an exceptionally well-run Belgian brewer. Most people in the U.S. have never heard of InBev, but they would recognize many of its brands, sold in 130 countries around the world. A formerly well-known American company like Anheuser Busch is now a Dutch company that has eliminated much of the waste from Budweiser's management team. Does that mean you shouldn't own it because it's no longer American?

That's where I think Buffett gets it wrong. Only in recent years has he begun to look overseas.

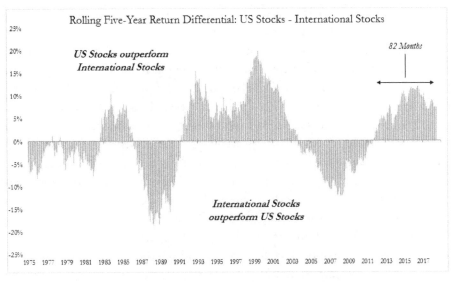

Source: Morningstar Direct. Data as of 6/30/2018.
Note: Int'l stocks are represented by MSCI World ex. U.S. from 1970 to 1988 and MSCI ACWI ex. U.S. from 1988 onward.

Fig. 12.8 U.S. vs International

Perhaps my perspective is different than his because of the influence of seeing the world as a C130 pilot, spending time in places like Africa, where I saw the impressive distribution of Coca-Cola. There's tremendous growth potential there and in India and China too, where they have growing populations. If you're the CEO of a company and all of your sales are based in the U.S., wouldn't it make sense for you to consider overseas distribution, where the potential for growth far outweighs that of the U.S.? Some of the great American banks are not highly regarded in Great Britain or Italy, where they have a bias towards their own banks. If, as an investor, you believe the statistics that indicate China is a growing economy and American banks don't have a strong presence in China, why would you only buy American bank stocks? You need to think globally.

Over the past eight years from 2011 through 2018, U.S. stocks hugely outperformed international stocks. Prior to that, just the opposite occurred, with U.S. stocks being massively outperformed by international stocks for a similar period of years. Conversely, from 1991 to 2003, U.S. stocks outperformed. From 1986 through 1991, international stocks held sway. As you can see from Figure 12.8, there's a cyclical theme here.

Within these cycles, mini trends occur where the longer-term trend is temporarily reversed. International stocks have just begun what appears to be a reversal of the past eight years. Will this trend continue or will U.S. stocks reassert themselves and continue to outperform? No one knows, which is why you want to make sure you get a free lunch: you want your portfolio to be diversified with both U.S. and international stocks.

I have clients who believe our portfolio should be heavier in U.S. stocks. Others believe we should increase our international holdings. It's truly an art trying to identify each client's risk tolerance and determine an effective asset allocation strategy. The only free lunch, however, is diversification. Industry pundits like Nick Murray agree with Buffett and favor having most if not all of your money in stocks because they generally provide the best performance. What I realized very early in my career, however, is that most investors can't tolerate the severe downturns the equity markets are subject to. Studies have shown that a balanced portfolio of stocks and bonds will provide a slightly lower return than one consisting of 100% stocks. Granted, ceding a 1% to 2% annual return over 30 years can make a significant difference in accumulation, but to pursue that additional return, equity investors must withstand the occasional horrific declines. Most investors do not have the financial wherewithal or psychological resilience to weather those episodes. That's why I believe portfolios should be diversified with bonds, specifically bonds which provide a higher rate of return than investment grade bonds. More about bonds in the next chapter.

Investing Versus Speculating

Writing along with David Dodd in their groundbreaking 1934 book, *Security Analysis*, Benjamin Graham offers a distinction between an investor and a speculator. "An investment operation is one which, upon thorough analysis, promises safety of principal and a satisfactory return. Operations not meeting those requirements are speculative."

Unlike investors who rely on assessing a company's fundamentals (i.e., earnings, P/E ratio, long term growth potential and whether it's selling for a reasonable valuation), speculators are busy trying to deduce what the stock or market is going to do in the short term.

In his later, seminal book, *The Intelligent Investor*, Graham identifies two types of investors: entrepreneurial and defensive. From a global macro standpoint, I'm what Graham would call a defensive investor, focusing on value stocks with good quality financial characteristics, using price to earnings as a primary valuation measure, and looking for larger companies with a consistent track record of earnings and dividend growth.

As a defensive investor, Graham suggests that even if you're incredibly bullish and believe the market is going to go up, you should never have more than 75% of your portfolio in stocks. Conversely, if you're especially bearish and believe the stock market is overvalued, you should never have less than 25% of your portfolio invested in stocks.

A defensive philosophy helps prevent getting too far ahead of yourself—getting ahead of your skis and thinking that the market is too undervalued or overvalued.

Economists—myself included—are all guessers when it comes to the markets.

Some of us are more scientific in our approach, but we are still employing best guestimates. The mathematicians have injected calculus, trying to create validity for their scientific guessing, but the reality is that economics is a human science, rooted in how you and I feel about things right now. That can quickly change, of course. If I am optimistic about the market, I might go out and buy a golf membership, or a new car, or hire a new employee. However, should a recession occur or geopolitical risk appear that threatens the economy, my rosy outlook can change in an instant, thereby altering my buying habits and subsequently global growth.

"One thing badly needed by investors — and a quality they rarely seem to have — is a sense of financial history. In nine companies out of ten, the factor of fluctuation has been a more dominant and important consideration in the matter of investment than has the factor of long-term growth or decline. Yet the market tends to greet each upsurge as if it were the beginning of an endless growth and each decline in earnings as if it presaged ultimate extinction."
Benjamin Graham

CHAPTER THIRTEEN

Bonds

Opportunistic Aardvarks Find Bigger Anthills

I believe one of the great investment misconceptions is that investors should buy the safest (lowest yield) bonds to offset the risk they take with the equity portion of their portfolio. That nostrum has it exactly backwards. Investors should be taking less risk with their equities and getting paid better for the risk they take with the fixed income portion of their portfolio.

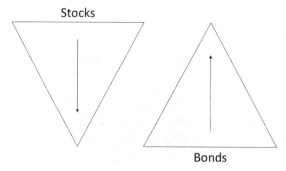

Fig.13.1 Inverse Triangles

Graphic 13.1 is a simplified depiction of the way I feel portfolio risk should be allocated between the two broad asset classes. The wider portion of each triangle represents the area in which most investors focus. Rather than investing where the masses gravitate, I believe one should instead invest where the minority of investors are converging.

Virtually every newly-minted MBA on Wall Street gravitates to the wider portion of the equity triangle, taking greater risk by eagerly gobbling up momentum stocks. There will always be a few of those companies that outperform but for every one that soars, there are many more that fail after their initial public offering. As discussed in previous chapters, I believe strongly that you should take less equity risk by avoiding momentum stocks and pursuing stocks that sell at reasonable valuations and pay dividends.

The bond market is the other way around. It's where to turn the equation on its head and take more risk, assuming you are being commensurately paid for the risk. You shouldn't be lending money to higher rated companies (especially for long durations) unless you are being adequately compensated, and you rarely are.

If the 10-year Treasury is at 2.5%, you're likely to receive little more than a 3% return for lending money to a safe corporation. Getting a .5% higher return over a riskless Treasury is not adequate compensation. Why would you lend money to Apple at a fraction of a percent higher than a riskless government bond and take the risk that a black swan event or deep recession could plunge even that apparently sound company into bankruptcy? [55] Granted, it's a low probability, but that's what bondholders in Lehman Brothers, General Motors, Pacific Gas & Electric, and Enron thought and they paid a heavy price for being wrong.

The overwhelming majority of bond investors consistently get it wrong. They always invest for safety; it's their nature to invest in the safest of bonds. Many are bears by nature. They're always worried and they purchase bonds which provide little to no return after taxes and inflation. They are so balance sheet driven that everything frightens them. Just as the growth mentality of stock peddlers causes them to blindly chase the sexy issues, bond investors often guarantee failure by acting like your crazy Uncle Joe who shows up for Thanksgiving and should be locked in the closet.

Many advisors get it completely wrong as well. In choosing money managers for their clients, they do a simple scatter plot, putting some of the equity portion of their portfolio into a growth manager, some into a value manager like Altrius, and the rest into a "safe" bond manager to manage the portfolio risk.

Investing large percentages of their clients' assets into lower risk bonds effectively guarantees failure for them. For example, assume interest rates are at their current level of 2.5%. After their 1% fee, taxes, and inflation, they're guaranteeing that their clients aren't going to retire as planned. What they are assuring is a negative rate of return after fees, taxes, and inflation. I constantly tell advisors that they have to take a little more risk. Instead of investing with fixed income managers focused on balance sheet risk, they should be looking for those analyzing the cash flow of a company. If a balance sheet is a bit stressed, not as pristine as they might like, that's okay — as long as the company's cash flow is sound. I often refer them to the big picture of the triangle graphic, suggesting that in the upside down triangle (stocks), they should be taking less risk in terms of volatility. In the bottom triangle (bonds), they should be taking more risk to be compensated properly for risks that they don't usually consider, which is those black swan type events that happen or deeper recession events that naturally occur at times. At that point, the bonds they felt were safe may turn out to default.

Rating Agency Miscalculations

Another major contributor to the investment misconceptions about bonds is the rating agency industry. After the financial crisis, wherein the rating agencies got it so wrong, many investors realized they could not rely on agency ratings. I've been agnostic towards the rating agencies since well before the financial crisis, taking advantage of fixed income pricing inefficiencies soon after founding my firm in 1997. I believe it best to ignore them other than when they downgrade a company, in which case I'm often looking at the issue as a potential purchase as many institutional managers who are bound by the agency's ratings become forced sellers.

When a bond is downgraded by a major rating agency like Moody's, Fitch or Standard & Poor's, the market typically reacts in knee-jerk fashion and the bond often experiences a sell off. In many cases, little has materially changed financially at the company. Its probability of default may have increased a fraction of a percentage but the prospect for a bankruptcy typically remains minimal after a downgrade.

The ramifications of a rating agency downgrade can be widespread. The investment policy statements of many large institutions, trust funds, and endowments mandate that the manager not invest in any bonds that are less than investment grade rated, meaning a rating of no lower than BBB- or Baa, depending on the agency. The impact of a downgrade and subsequent selloff is illustrated in the following graphic.[56]

Opportunity in Institutional Liquidations

Insurance companies hold over one third of outstanding investment grade bonds, while at the same time they are subject to regulations prohibiting or imposing large capital requirements on high yield bonds. Downgrades can create opportunities to acquire assets at depressed prices.

Insurer Selling by Risk-Based Capital Requirements

Median Cumulative Abnormal Returns Around Credit Downgrade

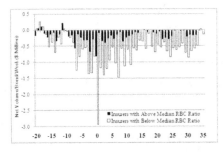
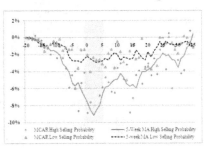

Source: Regulatory Pressure and Fire Sales in the Corporate Bond Market, Andrew Ellul, Chotibhak Jotikasthira, and Christian T. Lundblad (2011)

Fig. 13.2: Opportunity in Institutional Liquidations

Once a company is downgraded, these portfolio managers are forced to sell off their holdings — simply because someone at a credit rating agency has decided that it's not BBB-worthy anymore. Thus, the bond sells off but in most cases, eventually returns to its price pre-downgrade. Again, nothing of major significance has changed with the company as institutional managers are forced to sell it. When this happens, as a contrarian value investor, I'm usually a buyer. Others may be panic selling, but my analysis tells me that little has changed. It doesn't matter that an agency analyst has downgraded the company from BBB- to BB+, the market already knew that and the issue has usually already declined in price.

I'm very fortunate to have the trust of my clients and I am not constrained by an insistence that I only buy investment grade bonds. I have the freedom to seek the best risk/reward trade off across the credit spectrum and yield curve while opportunistically investing in inefficient circumstances. I'm able to be opportunistic because I am unconstrained by the investment policy strictures foisted upon other fixed income managers.

Credit Agency Role in the Financial Crisis

An examination of the causes for the financial crisis of 2008-09 reveals a long list of enablers. Politicians from both parties contributed to the disaster, whether the disembowelment of the Glass Steagall Act separating commercial and investment banking, the noble but misguided gesture of wanting everyone in America to be a home owner, or the tax code changes that encouraged home flipping. [57] But a major contributor was the rating agency industry that bestowed AAA ratings on collateralized debt obligations (CDOs), doing so simply because a single tranche of the structured product contained higher quality securities, and ignoring the remainder of the pooled securities, many of which were mortgages on dilapidated properties or unqualified buyers.

The banks and hedge fund managers were also largely complicit, using levered CDOs to enhance their returns and erroneous assumptions that real estate prices would climb endlessly. Financial institutions peddled the CDOs as "safe" AAA investments and institutional investors eagerly purchased them, viewing them as a free lunch and failing to understand what they contained. Finally, when some began to question the pricing and what these products actually contained, the world fell apart. Real estate prices plunged, investors walked away, and the models that said real estate would continue to go up 4% a year, even when it's overpriced, collapsed.

The rating agencies were the bedrock of this error in judgement however, as it was their AAA imprimatur on these hodgepodges that provided the necessary perception that they were safe, allowing banks and brokers to hawk them to trusting investors.

The agencies' inability to discern the flimsiness of those "investment grade" mortgage-backed securities was one reason for the implosion of that system in 2008 when it became apparent that those trillions of dollars of securities and their derivatives were worth a lot less than it seemed. Yet for all the reforms since then, the ratings agencies remain largely untouched. That's because those ratings underpin almost every major investment decision by every major institution in the world. Often, those institutions – from pension plans to sovereign wealth funds to companies themselves – cannot invest in bonds that are less than investment grade as determined by those agencies. It is a perfect "pass the buck" system and allows institutional investors to evade some responsibility if their decisions prove wrong. [58]

It is fair to say that the average and even above average investor relied on these ratings as trustworthy information provided from an agency which is strongly encouraged by the government. Further, these agencies often acted on information provided by the companies they were rating and not confirming the information with third-party resources, thus not ensuring the accuracy and integrity of the information they were using while calculating ratings. Conflicts of interests only made things worse by compounding the problems of the competency of these ratings and their trustworthiness.

The entire business model with which the big agencies operated presented immediate conflicts of interest. The rating agencies would be paid by companies who wanted their instruments rated. Because there is more than one agency to rate financial instruments, the companies could now shop for a better rating amongst the competing agencies. In turn, these agencies were competing for the largest market share in the ratings industry. Therefore, to gain more share, the agencies were often providing favorable ratings to these companies and their instruments to gain their business and add to the agency's market share.[59]

Sebastian Mallaby is the Paul A. Volcker senior fellow for international economics at the Council on Foreign Relations (CFR). He argues that government regulation is unlikely to solve the conflicts inherent in credit rating agencies, particularly when it comes to sovereign debt. *The best way to counter the monopolistic power of the Big Three, he argues, is for investors to stop giving their ratings so much weight.* "The reason why the subprime bubble could happen, or the reason why the European sovereign debt crisis can happen is, largely, that very blind investors bought bonds relying on ratings, and [didn't do] their own homework about what the real credit risk was in the bonds."[60]

This is one reason why I don't trust rating agencies, and a few other investors have now finally come to realize they are either incompetent or have sold out to the companies they purport to objectively rate.

What's fascinating is how often the rating agencies are so wrong about the companies they analyze, and that the emerging phenomenon is a general downgrading of issues in an attempt to salvage agency reputations after a company's debt sells off in price. They are now much more conservative in their analyses, not unlike home appraisers.

"People lost their jobs because the credit rating agencies didn't do the only job they're supposed to have, the only job they had, which is to give accurate, objective ratings to financial products."

Al Franken

How Will Your Clients Retire?

I continually wonder why advisors or institutional investors have their clients in Treasuries or other low-interest-paying fixed income securities in the current interest rate environment. I recall the CIO of an advisory firm who was directing his salespeople to recommend Invesco BulletShares ETFs. When I asked the CIO and his advisors if they knew what the yield was on the shares they were recommending, there were a lot of blank stares in the room. The CIO said he thought they were paying 4%. I told him he was mistaken and showed him that the BulletShares he was recommending were paying 2.25% at that time. I then displayed the securities the ETF contained, primarily investment grade bonds from some of America's and the world's largest, safest companies. Again, how can the clients of this advisory firm expect to retire when the bond funds they are recommending to their clients are yielding 2.25% annually? After the firm's 1% management fee, roughly 33% in taxes, and inflation of approximately another 2%, what's left for their clients? Certainly not enough to provide retirement income.

So why would you invest in investment grade bonds, particularly in a low interest rate environment? The answer is you shouldn't. You should be compensated for the risk that you're taking. It would be an extremely rare economic circumstance for me to purchase a bond yielding 2.5% or 3%. As a financial advisor, why would you recommend something with a yield that guarantees failure for your clients?

Well rated, investment grade corporate bonds typically don't offer much more yield than treasuries. For example, JP Morgan currently has over $300 billion in debt spread among almost 20,000 issues. A one year JP Morgan bond is yielding 2.4% with a one year Treasury bill currently at 2.2%. Why would I lend money to JP Morgan and only get .2% more return than a purportedly less risky Treasury? That makes no sense. Should we have another banking crisis, JP Morgan's debt would certainly sell off significantly as it did during the financial crisis. Of note, it was during the financial crisis that I was purchasing numerous banks with yields to maturity well over 20%, believing the opportunity presented a fat pitch moment.

I'm looking for value. I'm not going to pay more than I think an issue is worth. Thanks to the credit rating agencies who make decisions to downgrade companies, I get to be opportunistic and pursue the best risk/reward from the entire credit spectrum. During the financial crisis, I saw opportunity in the distressed banking sector because I believed the federal government would have to support the banking system. While others were scrambling to unload their bank issues, I seized upon what proved to be a rewarding contrarian opportunity.

High Yield Bond Opportunities

I'm continually probing sectors that most others avoid because it's where the opportunities reside and where one is getting paid for the risk. It's distressed value investing. Typically, the yield on high yield bonds is 4%-5% more than a Treasury bond of equal duration. In an environment with potentially rising interest rates, such as we are currently experiencing, I keep the durations short. I've always believed it generally best to keep durations between 2 to 4 years to protect against interest rate risk and have done so since the firm's founding. Duration is expressed as a number of years and is a measure of the sensitivity of the price — the value of principal — of a fixed-income investment to a change in interest rates.

Bond prices have an inverse relationship with interest rates. Therefore, declining interest rates indicate bond prices are likely to rise, while rising interest rates indicate bond prices are likely to fall. When interest rates rise, investors sell off their now lower priced issues. This often pushes the price of these bonds below par — a term describing a bond whose market price is below its face value or principal value, usually $1,000. As bond prices are quoted as a percentage of face value, a price below par would typically be anything less than 100.

An example of a circumstance and company in which I like to invest would be the rental car industry and specifically, Avis Budget Group, located here in New Jersey. Many investors fear that rental car companies are going out of business that everything will be self-driving and Uber will dominate the industry. That is, of course, a possibility to consider when weighing the risks. However, if you're a businessperson travelling to an area located a distance from a major airport, you're likely to rent a car to get around, even should that rental car be self-driven in the future. I have offices in New Jersey and North Carolina. If I have to fly into Raleigh and give presentations in Charlotte and Columbia, then return to my office in New Bern, renting a car is more economical and efficient than taking a taxi or mass transit, which isn't readily available.

Avis's debt is currently paying approximately 6% for a bond maturing in 2023. I'm getting paid for the risk — 3.25% more than a Treasury note of equal duration. Is there a chance that Avis Budget goes bankrupt over the next five years? Sure. Can I tell you what Moody's rating is on Budget? To use a movie line, "Frankly, my dear, I don't give a damn." The market gives me an implied rating which is more accurate because it's based on the price of the issue.

Better in Rising Rate Environment

From a risk perspective, my bond analysis process — like the stock analysis — still begins from a global macro perspective. I'm looking at the macro trends to find investment opportunities.

High yield bonds traditionally do better than investment grade bonds in a rising interest rate environment, such as we are currently experiencing. See the following graphic for an illustration of this.

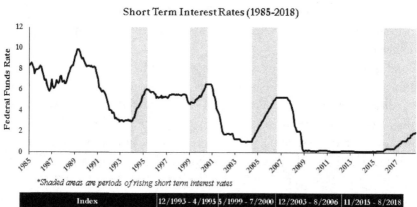

Bond Returns in Rising Interest Rate Environments

Short Term Interest Rates (1985-2018)

Shaded areas are periods of rising short term interest rates

Index	12/1993 - 4/1995	5/1999 - 7/2000	12/2003 - 8/2006	11/2015 - 8/2018
Credit Suisse HY Index	5.47%	(1.03%)	8.13%	7.45%
Barclays US Agg Bond Index	2.78%	3.39%	3.63%	1.62%
Barclays US Treasury Index	2.01%	4.12%	3.14%	0.71%
Barclays US Govt/Credit 1-3 Yr Index	3.71%	4.60%	2.32%	0.81%

Source: Federal Reserve Bank of St. Louis; Morningstar Direct

Fig. 13.3: Returns in Rising Rate Environments

When things are going well, corporations and individuals spend more money. Businesses experience greater profitability and thereby devote more to marketing, capital investments, employees, and travel to see prospects. Thus, they rent cars more often. As the economy heats up, the Federal Reserve raises interest rates to keep inflation at an acceptable level. This action is generally a negative outcome for safer, investment grade bonds. For example, if you purchased a 30-year bond at 3% and the Fed raises rates, investors can now get the same duration bond paying approximately 4%; thus, you've just lost 1% a year. Your $100k investment might now be worth only $70k. If you hold your bond to maturity, you'll get your $100k back but you're only going to earn $3k annually in an environment where the newer bond would have earned you $4k a year. Over 30 years, that's a substantial amount of lost interest. If you want to sell your bond, you have to compensate the buyer for the lower interest rate by offering a discount, so your bond may only be worth $70k.

High-yield bonds are not as interest rate sensitive. The reason? Let's go back and look at Avis Budget. Business is better because more people are renting cars; their balance sheet is also getting healthier. When their current high-yield bond comes due (or they call it back and pay it down), they can now qualify to borrow at a lower interest rate, which saves them money. An analogy would be an individual with poor credit having to borrow from a used car dealer at 10%. If his financial condition improves years later, he will be able to refinance at a bank for 7%. And while his interest rate has gone down because of his improved financial position, the bank's best customers may have to pay a higher interest rate because the Fed raised rates.

Thus, high-yield bonds like Avis Budget are not as interest rate sensitive as investment grade corporate bonds and treasuries, especially as you go further out on the yield curve. A yield curve is a line that plots the interest rates, at a set point in time, of bonds having equal credit quality but differing maturity dates. The most frequently reported yield curve compares the three-month, two-year, five-year, ten-year and 30-year U S Treasury debt.

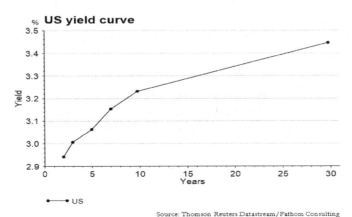

Source: Thomson Reuters Datastream/Fathom Consulting

Fig.13.4: Yield Curve

The shape of the yield curve gives an idea of future interest rate changes and economic activity. A normal yield curve is one in which longer maturity bonds have higher yields compared to shorter-term bonds due to the risks associated with time. An inverted yield curve is one in which the shorter-term yields are higher than the longer-term yields, which can be a sign of a potential recession. In a flat or humped yield curve, the shorter- and longer-term yields are very close to each other, which is often a predictor of an economic transition.[61]

There will be occasional knee-jerk sell offs of high yield bonds when investors panic because interest rates are rising rapidly, such as what happened during the summer of 2013 or when the economy goes into a recessionary period because high yield is more sensitive to the economy.

Incidentally, this is why owning individual bonds are preferable to owning a mutual fund. Let's say a broker has her clients in a high yield bond fund which declines 15%. Her clients are in a panic. She calls me to liquidate her clients' shares in the mutual fund — forcing me to sell bonds in the fund to pay out shareholders at depressed prices — thereby hurting everyone in the fund. This is a realized loss which may or may not be recovered due to the fund's open end structure and limits my ability to mitigate interest rate risk.

The broker's actions hurt everyone in this open end mutual fund because of the forced liquidation at distressed prices. If you or I own one of the particular bonds in the mutual fund outright in a separate account like we do for our clients, we will see the price go down because some panicked advisor or investor sold it; however, we shouldn't be bothered. We will own the position(s) for a fixed period of years. As long as the companies don't go bankrupt, we're going to continue to earn interest from the bond's coupon regardless of price fluctuations. In addition, we will receive par value for the bond when it matures assuming it doesn't default.

Of course, I could misjudge the credit risk and we can (and will) experience bankruptcies. That's why I don't use leverage, nor take significant positions in any one company in our portfolio. In addition, we continually stress test our portfolios at various default and recovery rate scenarios to determine our worst case performance in order to manage portfolio risk and assist with making sound macro decisions. More about stress testing later in this chapter.

Defaults Are Part of the Equation

Mathematical default models are just estimates. While the equations are complex and provide some guidance, making judgements on a particular issue is as much art as science. It takes experience to know what to invest in and what to avoid. No one is right all the time. When investing in high-yield (junk) bonds, one will always experience defaults and I've certainly not been immune to making mistakes in the 20+ years I've been managing money. Though I've certainly learned from my mistakes, I'll continue to make them. Growing comfortable in the uncomfortableness of investing, particularly in high-yield bonds, is a necessary investment trait.

Fixed income managers are balance sheet driven bears. They want to see perfect balance sheets, like Apple. But Apple doesn't need to borrow money; it has plenty of cash on its balance sheets. Banks are in the business of lending money to people who don't need money lent to them. Banks call me regularly to offer loans, yet I don't need to borrow money. I'm the type of client banks want: a low-risk investment.

Fixed income managers are always running scared. Like banks, they want the safest investments. I believe these managers are looking at the wrong financial statement and not getting paid for the risk. Instead of scrutinizing balance sheets, they should be paying more attention to income statements and cash flow.

A company can have too much leverage from which it can't recover, which is what happened to Toys R Us after it was purchased by Bain Capital, KKR & Company, and Vornado Realty Trust. I don't have much affection for private equity firms when they lever their purchases too meaningfully after purchasing them. They take a good company, often using too much leverage so they can pull out their massive fees, then pile on so much debt the company can no longer compete effectively and is eventually forced into bankruptcy. That's essentially what happened with Toys R Us headquartered in my home town of Wayne, New Jersey. The company had often teetered on the verge of bankruptcy since the 70's but had always survived. I'm certain it broke the founder's heart as he died soon after the company was forced into bankruptcy.

Even when defaults occur, bond investors generally don't lose 100% of the principal value of the bond as defaulted bonds usually have some salvage value. Sometimes defaults take the form of a suspension of coupon payments. Such bonds are said to be trading flat. If coupon payments are resumed, the price of the bonds may recover significantly. Bondholders may also benefit from the sale of assets of issuers under bankruptcy proceedings. Finally, under rarer circumstances, some bankrupt companies emerge successfully from bankruptcy proceedings, leading to larger recovery values.

The Unconstrained Process

Maintaining a global macro perspective, I look for issues that offer an attractive yield/spread relative to a similar duration treasury. Credit spreads are the differences in yield between two debt securities with differences in credit quality. A debt security with a higher credit quality sells at a higher price (and inversely a lower yield) compared to a similarly dated security of poorer credit quality.

Screening the market daily produces a list of potential bonds, which is reduced through analysis (see following graphic) to a buy list of securities which may present opportunities. As the market often speaks before the rating agencies do, buy and sell decisions are based on Altrius' criteria which includes my top-down, global macro perspective, coupled with a bottom-up, value driven security analysis process.

Unconstrained Fixed Income Process

Top down strategy employed to identify the most compelling portfolio positioning and opportunity set:	Bottom up process seeks to identify companies selling below their intrinsic value:	Invest unconstrained primarily in U.S. dollar-denominated investment grade and high yield bonds:
GLOBAL MACRO TOP DOWN PERSPECTIVE DRIVES INITIAL UNIVERSE	**VALUE** BOTTOM UP VALUE DRIVEN INVESTMENT ANALYSIS DRIVES SECURITY SELECTION	**TOTAL RETURN** FOCUSED ON ACHIEVING HIGHEST TOTAL RETURN WITHIN ACCEPTABLE LEVELS OF RISK
• Yield Curve Positioning • Sector Rotation • Duration • Credit Risk	• Income Statement Driven • Cash Flow Focused • Seeking Undervalued Securities • Seeking Above Average Income • Screening for Yield: Seeking 3-5% above the 5 yr treasury	• Invest in government securities, corporate bonds, mortgage backed and asset backed securities diversified across sectors. • Seek to attain an attractive yield/spread relative to a five year treasury within acceptable levels of portfolio risk.

Fig. 13.5: Unconstrained Process

We screen for securities that provide a reasonable yield to compensate for the risks of inflation, rising interest rates, and potential loss of principal. Income statements and cash flow metrics are emphasized, as well as management's competence and the company's ability to service and pay back debt. The unconstrained approach allows me to move freely throughout the credit structure to find the best value based on the market environment and the issue's credit risk/reward profile. As I previously mentioned, I do not rely on credit agency ratings to determine intrinsic value or the credit's opportunity for success. Because investment policy statements often force investment grade managers to sell downgraded bonds, we often find significant opportunities in the BBB- through CCC+ credit range.

Bond Risk Scenario Analysis

Just as I do a scenario analysis for stocks, I do a similar analysis for the fixed income asset class (see graphic that follows).

Over the past 30 years, defaults for high yields have averaged about 4% a year though certainly spiking higher during recessionary periods. For the purpose of a worst-case scenario analysis, I use the default rates which occurred as I was graduating from the Naval Academy in 1991 which experienced greater default rates than even the financial crisis. At the time of the savings and loan crisis of the early 90's, high yield bonds experienced approximately 30% default rates over a roughly four-year period. We also stress test a severe bear case entailing a 40% default rate over the same period, to determine a worst-case rate of return under such drastic circumstances.

Total Return through Risk/Reward

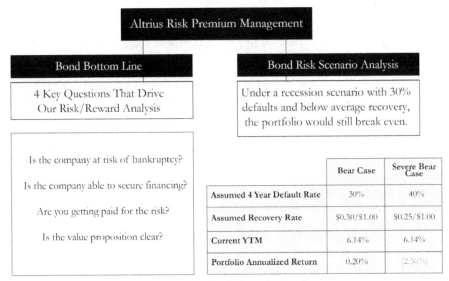

Fig. 13.6: Bond Risk Scenario Analysis

The chart assumes a roughly 6% annualized return on the high yield bonds in the portfolio. If we suffer 30% defaults over a four-year period, the portfolio would still provide an effectively flat rate of return, much like having your money in a savings account today. What if 40% of those companies go bankrupt and we only recover 25 cents on the dollar? There would be an annualized loss (-2.36%), but certainly not a catastrophic one.

So, as an unconstrained fixed income investor, it's important to remind oneself of the worst case scenario to resist the urge to sell distressed bond holdings in your portfolio when suffering through inevitable market corrections and economic recessions. Moving to cash by panic selling, generally only guarantees locking in losses, while holding onto your positions may lead to at worst the return you would achieve in a bank savings account.

Less Risky Than Stocks

Investors, and even financial advisors, often tell me they are afraid to put their clients into high-yield bonds because they are "too risky." Meanwhile, the same advisors have their clients invested in stocks, which, by any mathematical measure in finance — whether beta or standard deviation, which the economists utilize — are riskier. I repeat, stocks are riskier than high-yield bonds. The following graphic illustrates that mathematical fact.

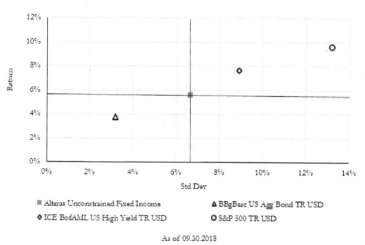

High Yield Bonds Have Provided Equity-Like Risk-Adjusted Returns

Over the past 15 years, our high yield strategy has produced more than half the return of equities with only half the risk, as measured by standard deviation. This corresponds to a return per unit of risk (annualized return divided by annualized volatility) of 0.84 for the Unconstrained Fixed Income strategy, versus 0.73 for the S&P 500.

Fig.13.7: Equity-Like Risk Adjusted Returns

As you can see, over the past 15 years, a high-yield strategy has produced equity-like returns with less risk as measured by standard deviation.

Over the past two decades, high-yield bonds have also experienced lower volatility than the S&P 500, as measured by standard deviation over monthly 3-year rolling periods.

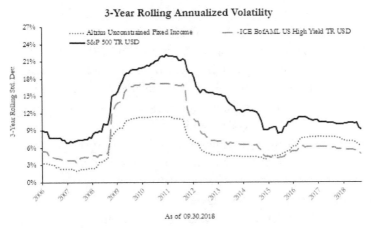

High Yield Bonds Have Been Less Volatile
Than Equities

Since 2000, high yield bonds have experienced lower volatility than the S&P 500, as measured by standard deviation over monthly 3-year rolling periods.

3-Year Rolling Annualized Volatility

As of 09.30.2018

Fig. 13.8: High Yield Bonds Less Volatile

Those who say high-yield bonds are too risky cite defaults, but there's no way to achieve a satisfactory rate of return among the fixed income asset class without having occasional defaults. If I invest in something safe like a U.S. Treasury, my clients are going to receive the same miniscule return many bond managers deliver, a return that virtually guarantees they won't be able to retire and maintain their lifestyle, assuming they can retire at all. If you are a client with a million dollar portfolio and I'm a safe bond manager getting you a 2% annual return, can you live on $20,000 a year (less after taxes and inflation)?

If you have $10 million in assets, you may be able to invest very conservatively in nothing but safe bonds should you choose to live on the after-tax proceeds of the bonds. However, inflation will still erode your principal every year. If you don't have the luxury of adequate assets to sustain a lifestyle from just 1 to 1 ½% of the assets, you better get comfortable with the idea of investing in high-yield companies. If you are among those who have diligently saved a million dollar retirement portfolio and you want to live a comfortable retirement and spend $40,000 a year in addition to your Social Security, I suggest investing in high-yield bonds and dividend paying stocks as the best means to potentially achieve that end.

Individual Bonds vs Bond Funds

I received a letter from a client inquiring about bond funds and individual bonds. He referred me to an article in Barron's about oversold bond funds paying ridiculously high rates of return with equally ridiculous discounts from net asset value. He asked why I was not buying other people's funds that have declined in value versus buying the individual debt issues?

He suggested that if I would focus my analysis on these high-yield, closed-end junk funds versus individual bonds, I could make a lot more money for my investors and my firm, even after paying the expenses of these closed-end funds.

I responded that his assumptions and conclusion — as well as the Barron's article — are incorrect for several reasons.

For one, yield isn't the only consideration for investment as one may achieve a higher rate of return due to total return from a discounted issue.

Second, the closed-end funds he referred to achieve a higher yield by using leverage. I could certainly use leverage in an effort to boost yield but that strategy is a dangerous proposition that can lead to much greater losses as discussed in a previous chapter.

Third, investing in mutual funds does not allow me to control interest rate risk. If one of our clients panic sells a position(s), the rest of our clients may see a price decline in the issue due to the sale of the bond, but as long as the issue doesn't default before maturity, our clients holding individual bonds will receive continued interest payments and their principal. When we have to sell the same issue for mutual fund clients, however, it in turn hurts all clients in the fund. In the case of an open-ended fund, it often leads to additional redemption requests, in turn creating a vicious cycle in which mutual fund investors may not receive their principal back. Thus, the mutual fund investor not only takes on credit risk, but also interest rate risk. Though closed-end funds are less susceptible to interest rate risk (though not immune, particularly when using leverage), they also are priced by secondary demand and contain other risks.

It would be infinitely easier to do what most financial advisory firms do by simply charging their clients 3/4% to 1% for merely researching other money managers. I believe, however, that the benefits that accrue to our clients for owning individual bonds and stocks are worth the additional staff and effort.

The Doctor Has Cash Flow

I like to think of distressed companies as if I were investing in a young doctor. He typically comes out of medical school with a ton of debt. After joining a practice, he has job security with a $500,000 salary and purchases a $1 million home. He has excellent cash flow, but a good amount of debt and new bills to match. A bank is more than happy to loan the young doctor the money to purchase the million dollar home due to his excellent salary and job security. However, let's assume the loan is a five-year adjustable rate mortgage and when it comes due, that the bank demands payment on the remaining principal, asking him for $900,000. The doctor would, of course, reply to the bank that he has the cash flow to continue to make his monthly mortgage payments (which are mostly interest in the early years), but that he hasn't yet had the time to save enough to repay the bank in full and desires to enter into another five-year adjustable rate or longer-term fixed rate mortgage.

The bank, of course, doesn't ever demand payment in full of the five-year adjustable rate mortgage. Instead, they simply roll the loan over into another loan. The bank doesn't want the house; they want the doctor to keep making payments so they can profit from the interest. And they're confident it's a safe loan because the doctor has adequate cash flow to pay his interest expenses. Most high yield companies are structured in the same manner as this young doctor as they have sound cash flow, but don't have the ability to pay off all of their debt if investment banks don't continue to roll it into another issue when their bond matures. Frankly, most small businesses which drive our American economy, and many large, publicly traded companies, are in the same circumstance.

The media and many fixed income investment managers and analysts often fret over what they describe as the "debt cliff" that's coming when Avis Budget and other high yield companies are confronted with mounting debt redemptions. I've been through plenty of these cliffs in my career. I liken the supposed debt cliff to the looming debt payments of all the doctors graduating from medical school in a single year. You know what? They'll be fine under most circumstances. If interest rates go up from 5.9% to 7.2%, they have to pay a little more interest but their cash flow will accommodate that. The commercial bank is not going to call the doctor's loan, just as the investment banks don't want to lose that $500 million they loaned a rental car company. They're going to roll the debt into a new bond unless something catastrophic has happened to the industry (such as the coal industry during the energy crisis of 2014-2015 when energy prices collapsed) or to the company itself.

The companies I like to invest in are like investing in doctors with great cash flow. Their balance sheets might be strained, but they've got consistent cash flow. They're a good risk; they're usually going to pay me back. Like the doctor and his $1 million home, most are not able to pay back a million in debt if they had to, but they're making enough to keep paying the interest on their debt and show a profit. The great majority of the companies I invest in have positive cash flow and interest coverage on their debt. They're able to service their debt and usually turn a profit.

Investing in Hope

When I speak of an investment in hope I refer to an investment in a company that doesn't have interest coverage. An example would be Sears, a company lacking even operating income but whose real estate holdings and brands such as Kenmore, Craftsman, and DieHard cushioned it against bankruptcy during the time in which we held the issue and gave enough hope for investment banks to continue to offer Sears a lifeline by extending its debt.

When purchasing companies that are an "investment in hope," it is generally a circumstance in which a turnaround or catalyst for change is necessary for the company to become profitable and to have interest coverage on their debt. Making such investments is even more art than science as the math rarely adds up.

It is under such circumstances in which one is often purchasing the debt at a steeper discount in order to be compensated for the risk, and the company's debt has often fallen significantly from par value, i.e., 80 cents on the dollar. Many individual investors don't understand how they are getting a higher rate of return than the coupon on the face value of the bond. They look at the coupon and say, "Wait a minute. When they initially borrowed money from the bank, they were only borrowing it at 7%. How am I getting a 12% return?"

The answer is that they're buying the bond at 80 cents on the dollar. If the company doesn't go bankrupt, investors will get 100 cents on the dollar back at maturity. They're going to make a 25% return ($20/$80) over the next five years in capital gains while also receiving the 7% interest payment each year. Add up the capital gain and the coupon and the investor receives a 12% annualized return.

Late each night, my kids see me sitting in front of a computer and wonder what I'm doing. I try to teach them about investing and get them interested in finance by pointing out stocks of the companies we own and bonds of companies to which we lend money. I explain to them how finance makes the world go around and that without it, industry and economies cannot grow. Whether you're financing a rental car company, a consumer goods producer or a doctor, finance is exciting and vital to capitalism.

Sometimes, the anthill overlooked by the other aardvarks contains the juiciest critters.

Section III

How to Become a Wealthy Aardvark

CHAPTER FOURTEEN

Making Smart Choices

The Aardvark Pays Himself First and Spends Wisely

Unlike the majority of Wall Street inhabitants whose interest in managing other people's money incubated in an Ivy League classroom, my fascination arose while I was serving in the military, helping young Marines wrestle with their financial issues.

As a lieutenant, you might think my biggest challenges were tactical in nature: charging up a hill or learning to fly the KC-130 Hercules. The reality, however, was that the biggest challenges most Marines faced were personal in nature, specifically issues related to family and money. The amount of time spent away from spouses was one cause of marital conflicts but money and finances were inevitably involved as well. Like the priest I never became, I found myself doing a great deal of counseling, particularly with young Marines learning to balance their military responsibilities with their personal commitments.

Young Marines, not unlike the fledgling members of the other branches of the military, often have a tough time managing money. Sometimes, they blow through whatever amount they make, which isn't a lot to start with. There's no shortage of financial predators happy to relieve them of their money. Virtually every temptation known to man resides outside the gates: car dealers, bookies, tattoo parlors, strip clubs, everything designed to separate Marines from their meager earnings.

Aside from the nefarious enticements, one of the biggest problems was the prosaic automobile. Young Marines I counseled had a remarkable ability to overspend on what should have been basic transportation. It was not uncommon for them to waste 40 or 50% of their salary on an option-laden Mustang or Camaro they had no business buying. A typical conversation I had with these young Marines was to ask them, "Lance Corporal Benatz, if I offered you an opportunity to invest 20k in my business and I told you the minute you walked out the door that your 20k was guaranteed to be worth no more than 15k, would you say that's a good investment?"

"No sir."

"What if I guaranteed you that 5 years from now, your 20k would be worth 10k? Would that sound any better?

"No sir. That would be a horrible investment, sir."

"Well, Lance Corporal, that's what your automobile is; a horrible investment. You may think it's a necessary evil and perhaps you do need a car, but do you need a brand new Mustang convertible that costs you half of what you earn as a Marine?"

This was a regular challenge I faced as a young Marine officer. It was my first taste of financial planning and its importance.

After establishing my professional practice, many of the personal and financial challenges I helped my clients work through were the same issues those young Marines faced. As people navigate the financial waters of their lives, they get married, have children, get divorced, get remarried, have more children, tackle college costs, relocate, lose their parents, change careers, build businesses, and grapple with taxes, all the while hopefully trying to save for retirement.

Spenders and Savers

This may be a bit of broad assessment, but in my experience, people tend to fall into two categories: savers and spenders. The big difference between the two is that savers are better able to distinguish between a want and a need, and make financial decisions with that in mind.

A long-time client of mine is a spender who, despite my continual cautions, can't resist splurging on virtually everything she buys or does. When I provided her with an accounting of the more than $2.5 million she has spent over the past fourteen years, she was surprised. I warned her that if she continues to spend at her current rate, she would likely deplete her assets by her early to mid 80's.

Her chances for not outliving her money would rise dramatically if she had the discipline to live on the $10,000 in dividends and interest her portfolio generates each month. Most people I know could live comfortably on $120,000 a year. *She is a classic spender.*

One of my other clients is a member of the greatest generation. Now in her eighties, she has several million in her portfolio but lives on $70k a year. Her portfolio earns well in excess of that amount but she refuses to spend beyond her self-imposed budget; she even double dips tea bags.

Her portfolio is conservatively allocated with just 30% invested in dividend producing stocks and the remainder in bonds. She could lose two-thirds of her portfolio and still be fine, yet she remains nervous about spending and the loss of principal. *She is the definition of a saver.*

The spender inherited her money. She's in little financial danger for the time being, but her spending will create a negative cascading effect as she dips into her principal and outstrips the approximate 4.5% of interest and dividend payments providing her with regular income.

A lot of people hope to spend their last dollar before death. I like to quip that it's not a problem: just tell me when you're going to die and I'll make sure you spend that last dollar.

That's the unknown. People say they want to frontload their spending in their earlier retirement years. The problem is a lot of people remain healthy and active well into their eighties and nineties. If a financial crisis or depression occurs, or even if we experience a normal recession, those who accelerate spending from age 55 to 75 will have a dramatically increased likelihood of running out of money before they die.

An oft suggested "Golden Rule of Retirement" is to live on no more than 4% of your assets annually. A common practice for money management firms is to toss their clients' retirement portfolios into an array of mutual funds and hope for enough appreciation to provide for that 4% withdrawal rate while also providing enough gains to stay ahead of the insidious impact of inflation and taxes over time.

I prefer to avoid investing in hope. Rather than relying on mutual fund appreciation, I suggest adhering to the Golden Rule by receiving your 4% annually through dividends and interest income. Over time, the portion of your portfolio invested in solid dividend paying companies should go up in value to help hedge against inflation and taxes.

Whether serving in the military or living in civilian life, there will always be financial predators trying to separate you from your money, trying to convince you that you should satisfy your wants, not just your needs. No matter what you look to buy, there's always an upgrade available. An airline upgrade, the automobile's all-leather interior, the even-bigger TV screen, the custom kitchen cabinets, even those $19.95 TV commercials offer upgraded versions. Be vigilant about your spending and aware of the difference between what you want and what you need.

Rethinking Retirement

I believe retirement needs to be rethought. People used to retire at 60 or 65 and be dead in a few years. In 1940, there were 159 workers for every Social Security beneficiary; by 1995 the ratio was down to 8.6.[62] Today, there are less than 3 workers for every recipient. Many people retire early now and they're living into their 80's and 90's. Medicine is doing remarkable things and people are living longer and longer. The common notion that retirement means no longer working may have been valid when the average lifespan was 65, but it's an outmoded concept in today's world. We are living longer and staying healthier for a longer portion of our lives. The down side is we need a lot more money to maintain a lifestyle throughout our lifetimes.

Doing nothing during retirement is not intellectually stimulating, nor is it healthy for your physical or emotional wellbeing. If you want to spend more in retirement, why not work a couple days a week or find work that you truly enjoy? Work is not a four-letter word. People tend to stay healthier when they're working.

Forget Budgeting

I cringe when I hear advisors tell their clients they need to be on a budget. In my experience, arguments over budgeting are one of the major causes of marital strife. Typically, one spouse is a saver, the other a spender. The two opposites are a recipe for ongoing conflict.

The first thing couples should do is agree on their goals. If a priority is to retire at age 65, work the numbers backwards. There is interactive software that makes this easy; couples can monitor their portfolios and see if they are on track for their goals in real time. It links them into their planning software. Most people have similar goals: they want to retire and live a certain lifestyle and spend their last dollar the day they die. I have some clients who place an emphasis on leaving a legacy but they are generally the exception.

Let's say a 40-year-old couple has a goal of having their retirement portfolio generate 50k a year by their retirement at age 65. It's relatively simple to work that backwards. Divide 50k by .04 (the Golden Rule of Retirement) and it's obvious the couple needs $1.25 million in assets in today's dollars. If we assume a 6% annual rate of return, the couple needs to save $1,800 each month to accumulate $1.25 million. This of course is a simple plan which doesn't include inflation and taxes so you will want to utilize more sophisticated software which includes these calculations along with the various type of retirement accounts available to you. Working closely with your financial and tax advisors will help with more detailed planning considerations.

The second most common goal among families is to provide for their children's education. Each parent has their own ideas about how best to do this: it's an individual decision. Some parents believe the kids should pay. That way, they appreciate it and work hard in college. Some parents may be of my mindset that the financial burden is very high and don't want their kids to work while in school so they have more time to focus on getting good grades. I have a contract that my kids sign. It says I will pay for four years and four years only. If they want to work through summers and strive to secure a master's degree during that period, that's fine. I'll pay for the Masters also if they can achieve it during a four year period. I show them a list of 25 of the most expensive colleges — Harvard, Princeton, Notre Dame, Wellesley — the schools that have the potential to open up some doors for them if they work hard while there.

I may consider paying 70k a year for these colleges provided my kids work hard enough during high school to get into them, which is tough nowadays. Otherwise, there are a lot of excellent schools whose cost is much more reasonable. I advise many of my clients who want to save for their kids' college expenses to do what I've done: open a 529 plan with a low expense ratio. I help them set it up and if they start to save $400 a month when their child is born, they would have made contributions of approximately $86,000. If you assume that your rate of return (i.e. 7%) is equal to the inflation rate of college (historically higher than the average inflation rate), you should have enough saved to pay for a good state school. The nice thing about 529 savings plans is that they're flexible while also allowing for tax free growth if used for higher education expenses. I'm currently paying out of pocket for my daughter to attend college with the goal of using her 529 savings for my grandchildren to take that burden off my daughter should she have children.

College expenses have escalated so rapidly. The government may have done students a disservice by offering such cheap loans. It's enabled colleges to continue to build and grow and keep raising tuitions at rates that are much higher than the inflation rate over the last few decades.

From a financial planning standpoint, that's it. After you put away X amount of dollars for the life you want to lead in retirement based upon your current age, and after you put away for your kid's college, have some fun. Spend your money. Don't worry about a budget. Dave Ramsey, Suze Orman, and others insist you must create a budget and do this and that. There are certainly some success stories of people who budget, but these are people who are generally already saving money. They simply need to know how much to save and how best to do it.

The spenders are a more difficult proposition. They first need to be forced to become savers. It's the old *Wealthy Barber* adage: pay yourself first, put away for your retirement, and live within your means. You pay your car payment and mortgage (or rent) every month. Likewise, pay for your kid's college every month if it is your desire to take that burden off them. Put away for your retirement every month, regardless. Write that check to your Roth IRA every month (if you are eligible), and invest it for the long term. Don't worry about day to day market volatility. Just let it go. People worry needlessly about everything from tariffs to West Nile Virus to Y2K. It's silly. What impact does what they are fretting about have on how many Nestle bars are consumed in China? Regardless of what's going on in the markets, Nestle is usually going to pay their dividend and grow their earnings over time. Presidents come and go but people around the world will still be drinking Pepsi. As a patriot, you can worry about these things but from capitalistic perspective, I really don't care.

"I spent half my money on gambling, alcohol, and wild women. The other half I wasted."
W.C. Fields

Pay Off Your Mortgage

It's all too common for financial advisors to recommend their clients not pay off their mortgage: "Joe, the interest rate on your mortgage is 4.5%. Don't pay it off, give me the money and I'll invest it for you in this annuity that pays 7%."

It's horrible advice. Advisors peddling annuities or other financial products have a conflict of interest. In fact, as a fiduciary, it's one of the few times I have a potential conflict of interest as well. Clients ask if they should pay off their mortgage or keep the mortgage and invest the money with me instead. If they're retired or within 5 years of retirement, I suggest they pay off the house. They may counter, "But Jim, you made me 7% over the last decade. We can beat the mortgage interest rate." That may be true, but when the next inevitable market correction occurs, clients will feel that much more secure with the knowledge that their home is paid off and no one can come and get it. It's true that their 500k invested in stocks and bonds (rather than in their home's principal) could produce 22k of income. However, when their million dollar portfolio is down to 800k during a recession and they're sweating their mortgage payment, they may not be emotionally capable of weathering that economic storm. I may be able to convince them to hang in; but in my experience, clients who have their home paid off are so much more emotionally stable in retirement than those who have to make a mortgage payment. I know I'm in the minority of financial advisors on this subject. However, the cynic in me believes that many financial advisors recommend their clients invest that 500k in an annuity that would make the advisor a 7% or $35,000 commission. I certainly wouldn't give that advice to my mother, nor place my mother's retirement savings in an annuity, so I'm not going to recommend it to a client.

What I tell my clients is that another 5k a year is not going to change my life. My best advice is not to invest that 500k with me but rather to pay off your mortgage and feel more secure during your retirement from that decision.

Your Home is Not an Investment

Don't think of your home as an asset because you're not going to be able to take the money out. Yes, reverse mortgages are one way to get some money out of the dirt, but they should only be utilized as a last ditch solution.

Whether you rent or own, your house provides an important need: shelter. It doesn't provide an income unless you rent out rooms. It's just money in the dirt. It can become an asset if, at some point, you're willing to sell it and downsize. But like most people, if you're going to live in your home for a long time or plan to trade up for a house that's bigger and more expensive, the house is not an asset; it's a necessary evil, like a car. When we review a client's net worth, it's nice to show them their investment portfolio is worth 3 million and their total net worth is 4 million. Banks love to see financials like that because they can lend you money and use your home as collateral...and snatch your home if you don't make the payments. Banks love to lend money to people who don't need to borrow money. A client can pull up our financial planning software and see that her net worth is an extra million because her million dollar home is paid off. But, there's no money there. The house can't pay her anything unless she takes out a reverse mortgage or downsizes that million dollar house into a 500k property. Now she has 500k that can potentially earn 4.5% a year in dividends and interest and possibly more with price appreciation.

A lot of people look down their nose at renters but renting is not a bad thing. I used to tell my Marines that all the time. Houses cost a ton of money. Something is always breaking. You're constantly changing the shingles on the roof, or painting the house, or replacing a water heater or air conditioner, or the basement is flooding. It's constant upkeep. It's nice to call the landlord and say "It's broken; fix it." People who say renting is throwing money out the window are wrong. You're getting shelter. You're paying money for a service — the roof over your head. That's not a bad thing. Members of the service who move around every couple of years have an easier time if they rent. Millennials, unlike their parents or grandparents who often remained at one job throughout their lives, need to stay mobile. If their employer transfers them across the country and they see it as a career opportunity, they don't want to be encumbered with a residence that may be underwater or in an area where it's hard to sell. Whereas if you're renting, you just pack and go. You're often better off with a lease and remaining mobile. You're getting shelter, a nice home, and the same school district for your kids. People who insist the American dream means owning your own home are wrong. You may be better off purchasing a home if you are able to stay in a particular location for many years, overcome the costs of ownership and if real estate prices appreciate in the particular geographic area in which you live. However, don't think that home ownership is the absolute end all as your particular circumstances must be considered.

I realize this may be a bit controversial but I believe people — and financial advisors — who think home ownership is mandatory have it wrong, especially in today's economy.

The aardvark stays mobile. If he runs out of anthills to raid in one neighborhood, he moves to another burrow and resumes his lifestyle in a new neighborhood with plentiful anthills.

Leasing Versus Buying a Car

Unless you live in a city with good mass transit, a car is one of those necessary evils; you need to be able to get around. I think whether to lease or buy your cars is largely a matter of your personality. If you're like me and you drive a 2000

Toyota Land Cruiser with 270,000 miles on the odometer, it makes sense to buy. You're going to hold onto it long enough to where it makes sense. If you're the type of person who wants — not needs — to get a new car every three years, you should lease.

People who are the spenders of the world believe it's important to drive a new car all the time. Of course, todays automobiles are so well made they can last for a decade or two with proper care, but spenders are prone to make completely irrational decisions. When the price of gas goes up a dollar, people rush to get rid of their SUVs and buy smaller, more fuel efficient cars, ostensibly to save money. I'll go through the math with them. They're going to trade in or sell their depreciated SUV for $15,000 and buy a Prius for $25,000. At a dollar a gallon higher price, they say they will save $50 a week on gas, or $2,500 a year. Well, they lost $5,000 selling their SUV because they sold it when gas prices had risen, plus they had to spend an additional $10,000 to get into the Prius. That's $15,000. At that rate, it will take them six years to recoup the cost of their purchase.

I can't tell you how many times I've heard that rationale. I need a new car because gas is too high or my car has a few dents or the new models have this or that feature I need. What they're doing is justifying their reason to buy a new car. You see this play out on a large scale when the price of oil is lower as Ford and General Motors sell a ton more of their higher margin SUV's and trucks.

The key is to know thyself. If you are a spender, someone who thinks he needs to drive the latest model, you're better off leasing because you're simply paying for depreciation. Don't think that you're throwing the money away any more than you would be renting a home versus buying.

Don't Sweat a Little Debt

Susie Orman, Dave Ramsey, and other financial evangelists often preach to avoid investing until all of your debt is paid off. I don't believe this advice makes sense because most people will always have some debt. You have to simultaneously attack debt and investment goals. This is particularly true during your younger, accumulation years since time is important for compounding to occur.

If an aardvark waited to attack an anthill until it was perfectly safe to do so, he would starve to death. If Marines waited to attack a hill until it was completely safe, they would never accomplish their mission. Instead, they optimize conditions for the attack, use air superiority to drop bombs on the enemy, lob artillery on them, and then charge up the hill. You have to attack the debt payments, try to knock down your debt, throw your credit cards into a drawer and don't use them until you can pay them off every month. Pay with cash as you will feel the burden of your expenses more strongly than when using plastic. Importantly however, don't ignore your investment goals while you're trying to become completely debt free.

I have a client with a multimillion dollar portfolio who opened a 100k home equity line of credit. Why? Because it was available. Here's a person who's supposed to be living on the 10k monthly generated by his $2.6 million portfolio. Why is it that's not enough? His home is paid off but he takes out a home equity loan so he can buy a new boat. He doesn't *need* a bigger boat; he *wants* a bigger boat. He should instead be living within his means.

Many baby boomers are unprepared for retirement. They spend too much. They're living longer and they'll have to work longer. Many who have saved little will to be forced to live within their means on Social Security. The fact that they haven't saved for retirement may not necessarily be a bad thing, however. Work is not a four-letter word. It's okay. From an economic viewpoint, I don't see that as a social ill. I always tease my children, telling them that they shouldn't plan on taking over the business unless they desire to work well into their 70's since I want to work until I'm at least 100!

Russo's Ritz-Carlton Rule for Second Homes

Here's another choice that usually makes no financial sense. I call it my Ritz-Carlton Rule in regard to second homes.

Let's say I decide to buy a vacation home. My family and I love to ski so I buy a second home in Jackson Hole, Wyoming or Aspen, Colorado, spending a million dollars for one of those properties. But I have kids in college, a thriving business and a busy life, so it's hard to get out to the property more than 3-4 times a year. Meanwhile, between the mortgage, upkeep and other expenses, I'm spending $80,000 a year for the place. At that annual expense, I could stay in a Ritz-Carlton anywhere in the world for 4-5 months out of the year. Most people of course don't use their vacation home often enough to justify the cost. I know people that own second homes who say the appreciation on their ski lodge or waterfront property will do nothing but go up. That end is unfortunately not always the case.

People want vacation homes, whether in Aspen, Ft. Lauderdale, Las Vegas or Palm Springs. However, I may get tired of going to the same place. I can stay at the Four Seasons in Jackson Hole or Ritz-Carlton in Aspen. Maybe I don't feel like skiing this year because it's been such a long winter. Maybe I'll go down to

Naples and stay at the Ritz there. If you aren't going to use that vacation home at least a few months out of the year, don't even consider buying it. Take $20,000 and go to Italy or Paris. Don't make the mistake of thinking that vacation home is going to go up in value. Not necessarily. That property may not appreciate at all. Spend your vacation money wisely. That's my Ritz-Carlton Rule.

Cut the Cord

It depresses me to see couples well into their 60's still taking care of their 30-something children. These are no longer children; they are adults that need to be taught self-reliance. I've seen seniors literally go broke because they can't say "no" to their kids. Often, it isn't until that happens and the children no longer receive money from the bankrupt parents that the children are forced to take control of their own destiny.

You should certainly help your children if you want when they are in dire need. Oftentimes, however, parents enable their spendthrift children by continually giving them money for their newest "emergency." It's often difficult to show tough love, but when children manipulate their parents and are continuously living off of them, they can't become self-sufficient adults. Parents who support their child's profligate actions often do so to the detriment of their own financial stability while also causing the child to learn potentially harmful financial behaviors.

One way to avoid this is to create a contract with your kids to help them become financially responsible at an early age. My kids understand they will not receive a large inheritance as I believe it could detract from a productive life. I want them to be accomplished on their own and to understand to live within their means in whatever occupation they find of value.

Teaching Your Children Financial Values

It's trite to say that one should "follow their passion"; however, each occupational choice has financial and emotional value and worth. One may have a great passion for painting, but must also understand that choosing that life may not bring great financial reward. One choosing the noble professions of nursing, teaching, police work, military service or fire-fighting may garner tremendous emotional value from their honorable work. Though not likely leading to untold riches, such occupations could provide a comfortable life including a possible pension. Another may choose an entrepreneurial endeavor with great potential financial reward, but such an occupational choice may also lead to failure or more time away from family.

There are certainly no guarantees in life. There are only opportunities. I try to teach my children that the choices they make now, how hard they work, what major they pursue in college or the type of career in which they desire to work all offer challenges and rewards. I don't know if there is such a thing as life-work balance. I prefer to call it life-work integration as we are always making decisions which are trade-offs of our time, energy, effort, and potential revenue. Understanding that there is no perfect life-work balance is just as important as understanding that you will likely never have enough money to accomplish all you may want in life. You need to make responsible financial decisions to live within your means and distinguish between your wants and needs.

My Three Bucket Approach

You have a variety of choices for retirement saving, depending on how different tax regimes and growth scenarios will impact your assets. As tax rates are subject to change over time, I recommend a three-pronged approach.

1. Your nonqualified assets held in a trust account, joint account or individual accounts are taxable as you go. Distributions from this bucket during retirement may be advantageous since principal contributions are distributed without taxes and appreciation on investments is taxed as capital gains, which is less than income tax levels.

2. Your tax deferred assets include traditional IRAs, SEP IRAs, Simple IRAs, and 401k's. These vehicles allow you to invest pre-tax dollars that can grow tax sheltered until withdrawn during retirement, at which time the funds are taxed as ordinary income, but you should be in a lower tax bracket than during your working years. For example, if you're making 100k, and you put 5k away into your IRA or 401k plan, you're only taxed on 95k. You save some money on current taxes and pay taxes only when you take the money out during retirement, hopefully in a lower bracket. Business owners have more options available. A Simplified Employee Pension (SEP) plan allows employers to set aside money in retirement accounts for themselves and their employees and may make sense for those

with few employees. A SEP does not have the startup and operating costs of a conventional retirement plan and allows for a contribution of up to 25% of each employee's pay up to a limit. For businesses with less than 100 employees, a Savings Incentive Match Plan for Employees (SIMPLE) IRA may be a good choice. It allows employees to contribute up to 3% of their pretax compensation and employers have the option of matching the employee contribution or contributing a fixed percentage of each employee's pay. It's an inexpensive option for small businesses as it typically doesn't require a third party administrator (TPA). 401k/Profit Sharing Plans are more complex and require third party plan administrators, but allow for large pre-tax contributions for the business owner and matching contributions for employees. As a business owner, it's essential to analyze a census of your employees and review each of these plans, along with your goals, to choose the best option. One potential pitfall with the tax-deferred bucket is placing all of your retirement assets into it. Many of my clients are doctors or business owners who have accumulated $2-4 million in their profit sharing 401k. When they retire and want annual withdrawals over a hundred thousand, they get hammered by taxes, often losing a third or more to the government.

3. The third bucket is the tax free bucket, where you can use a Roth IRA or a Roth 401k if available from your employer. If your modified adjusted gross income (MAGI) is less than a certain amount (currently $135,000 for singles, $199,000 for married couples) you can contribute to a Roth IRA, currently up to $5,500 annually, subject to certain restrictions. It's a wonderful way to accumulate retirement funds tax free. If you qualify for a Roth, use it.

Don't leave money on the table if you're an employee and your employer offers matching contributions. If you don't put any money in, you may lose the matching funds. Always take advantage of matching funds.

Choose Your Engine

Working closely with your accountant and financial advisor, determine what should go into each of your three buckets. I sometimes advise individuals to think of investment accounts as if they were automobiles. The buckets represent the chassis of your car, the shell of the vehicle that might take the form of a traditional or Roth IRA, 401K, or a regular account. The engine you choose for the shell is what propels the vehicle and determines how fast and reliably you can go. It could be a single-stroke, three cylinder engine in the form of CDs or treasury bonds, in which case your car is not going to go very fast. You may believe you're minimizing the chances for an accident but you risk having inflation and tax detours prevent you from ever getting to your destination.

A potentially faster engine option would be corporate bonds, a four cylinder alternative which offers more speed in the form of higher returns. You might consider a six cylinder engine like high yield bonds, which may produce equity-like returns with less risk than stocks. Lastly, you may desire a traditional V8 engine in the form of stocks which may provide the fastest speed and returns for your vehicle.

This portion of the book is not meant to be a comprehensive "how-to" for financial planning as I believe that life is continually shifting, as are tax laws. Who knows what taxes are going to be 10, 20 or 30 years from now? Congress could raise or lower them. Using my three bucket approach may give you the needed flexibility to minimize your tax burden while you accumulate, and distribute, assets for your retirement. Each person's circumstances and goals are unique, however, and I'm not going to make absolute statements (such as "everyone should have a trust or a Roth IRA") utilized by those shilling books or seminars. I'm obviously biased, but I believe that using tax, legal, and financial professionals as your economic team is the most prudent way in which to tackle these complex matters.

The aardvark never passes up a free meal. If there are ants crawling around on the ground that don't require dissecting an anthill to get at, he eagerly accepts the contribution.

Chapter 15

Perilous Practices

The Aardvark Avoids Anthills Near His Predator's
Hunting Ground

Sitting on Cash

I previously mentioned my issues with people like Suze Orman who make broad generalizations and absolute statements such as recommending people eliminate *all* their debt before they start investing. Another Orman nostrum is that *everyone* should have six months' salary put aside in a cash account. Listening to that advice, many would never get started investing. It may sound good but most people don't have two weeks' salary put aside, much less six months' income.

There is no "right" amount to have set aside; it's different for everyone. It should be based on what makes you comfortable. For example, my number is zero. I have job security so I don't need to save money for unemployment. Similarly, a lot of my clients own their own businesses or have stable government jobs and have little need to hold anything in cash beyond saving for a new roof or heating and air unit.

I believe you should invest on a regular monthly basis: Set your retirement, college, and any other long-term goals, then work the numbers backward to determine how much you need to invest monthly to reach your goals. And while I recommend you make investing a priority versus sitting on a certain amount of cash, I recognize there are people who enjoy a level of comfort by having cash on hand.

My dad, who was a stockbroker, always kept $10k in cash with a rubber band around it in his desk. I once asked him what he would say to a client who kept that much cash around? He replied, "I would tell them they're crazy!" I asked, "Why then do you keep so much cash in your desk?"

His response: "Because I like to look at it."

Personally, I rarely carry more than $100 with me, and I only carry that much because here in the New Jersey/New York area, there are a lot of businesses that only accept cash.

If you are one of those people who need (or like) to keep a substantial amount in cash or savings, you can go to bankrate.com and shop for the highest savings account rate for your money, which is still going to be a relatively low interest rate.

An exception would be if you anticipate needing a large amount of cash for a special need. For example, I had a client whose parent had to go into a nursing home with expenses totaling a quarter of her life's savings. He obviously needed to have money immediately available for his parent's needs. It's possible I could have invested it and earned his mother a better rate of return than his bank savings account, but as her need was immediate, it didn't make sense to risk a market correction taking away months of her nursing care. Similarly, my daughter in college and my son who will be entering college in two years have short-term financial needs. That money should be in cash, not invested in stocks, because the need is immediate and the stock market could correct tomorrow. I wouldn't want to lose an entire year or two of payments to my son's college because the stock market plunged.

I've had clients who wanted to leave money they were likely to need for short-term needs invested with me to achieve a potentially higher rate of return. However, when your need is short term or immediate, I believe you should take that money and put it in a cash account where it will be immediately available.

On the other hand, if you're in your working years and investing for your future retirement, or even if you're 60 years old and your joint life expectancy is 90, that's a long-term time horizon, in which case you shouldn't be trying to time the market. Stay invested, assuming you're comfortable with the amount of money you keep in cash for yourself.

If you're a professional, own a business or are a government employee or in the military, you probably don't need a large savings account. The U.S. government isn't likely to fire you. Get that money invested into your 401k, Roth IRA or thrift savings plan if you are in the military. If you have young kids who will be going to college, invest in stocks so it can potentially grow in a 529 plan. Maybe keep a couple thousand in cash in case you have to replace something expensive in your home or for an emergency.

A lot of my clients are making $200-$500k a year, so they don't need to keep 10k in a savings account for when the shingles blow off and they have to replace the roof; they simply write a check out of their income. There's less of a need to have a large savings account.

Though I have no idea what the short term brings, I am more concerned about those who were frightened by the financial crisis of 2008-09, moved to cash, and subsequently sat out one of the best bull markets of the past century. For my clients who, like me, don't need cash from their portfolio, we are able to utilize the dividends and interest payments to purchase more shares of stocks and bonds, which can be incredibly powerful to compounded return over time. For this reason, I worry little if our portfolios are up or down in any given year as it has a limited impact on the long-term success of my clients. Moreover, declining stock and bond prices do not impact the income of my clients who fund their retirement cash flow needs because dividend and interest payments remain relatively steady, whereas price fluctuations cause portfolio values to vary widely. A dividend-paying company's stock price may increase or decrease in value during any given year; however, the dividend payment, though not guaranteed, will generally remain steady and, importantly, may increase over time as the firm's earnings growth helps hedge against the insidious effects taxes and inflation can have on my clients' retirements.

Though my firm is compensated based upon our clients' portfolio values, their income does not change dramatically as long as the stocks we own continue to make their dividend payments and the bonds we hold continue to make interest payments. We will, however, experience defaults at times. This is a part of the risk to achieve potentially higher interest payments above the very low return currently available from cash/CDs/Treasury bills. Because a stock's price doesn't have an impact on the income it generates (in fact, the yield increases when the price declines), I actually prefer to have normal and healthy stock market corrections which enables us to utilize cash flow to repurchase shares at lower prices.

When your money is in the stock market and the market is down, you may feel like you've lost money, but you really haven't. At this point, it's a paper loss. A turnaround in the market can put you right back to breakeven and maybe even put a profit in your pocket. If you sell your holdings and move to cash, you lock in your losses. Such an action goes causes paper losses to become real losses with no hope of recovery. While paper losses don't feel good, long-term investors accept that the stock market rises and falls. Maintaining your positions when the market is down is the only way that your portfolio will have a chance to benefit when the market rebounds.[63]

Consult an Attorney

One downside of so much information being readily available on the Internet is that people start to think "do it yourself" applies to virtually everything. If you scroll enough self-diagnosis medical sites, you'll come away convinced you have everything from leprosy to Landau Kleffner Syndrome. DIY may be fine if you are building a doghouse, but too many people think it works for self-medication or legal matters.

You should always use an attorney when whatever you plan to do has potentially serious ramifications. There are so many little things that can trip you up on everything from business transactions to real estate closings to divorce. People try to save a few hundred or a few thousand dollars and end up costing themselves thousands or tens of thousands, not to mention the emotional consequences. The majority of my clients never think twice about enlisting the help of an attorney when necessary, but I know people who've made awful mistakes, or got advice using online document templates that were inadequate.

You may not be in love with attorneys but these people went to law school and have years of practice experience. They're going to be a little bit better at it than you.

I liken it to building a patio. Yes, I suppose I could build my own patio, but it's going to take me so long and I'm going to make so many mistakes, I'm probably going to wind up costing myself more than if I just hired someone who builds patios for a living. I'll discover the water isn't draining properly because I didn't get the pitch right, not to mention the stress I'll suffer from spending weekends for the next year trying to finish the job instead of doing fun things with my family.

It's the same with hiring attorneys. They know what you're trying to accomplish. They might have made some mistakes during their careers but the experience has taught them how to avoid the same mistakes. In my opinion, you should pay for the guy to put your patio together and the attorney to keep you from inadvertently doing something you will later regret.

I was a professional military pilot, but I don't fly my own plane when I travel between offices or visit clients. I'm experienced enough to know that I don't have the time to fly enough hours each month to stay current and could very well kill myself and my family. So many people who can afford their own planes should not be flying them. Private pilots kill themselves all the time because they think they have the requisite skills to do so. Whether medicine, legal or travel, use a professional. Don't be penny wise and pound foolish.

The same holds true for a professional investment manager. You may have the time to continually perform the research and analysis necessary to manage your own portfolio, but do you have the experience and requisite training to do so? People looking to learn how to invest sometimes ask if I would teach them how to do so. However, it takes a minimum of three years for a new associate to apprentice with me and become fundamentally competent — and many more years to have the requisite experience and acumen. Though these associates have studied economics and finance for their undergraduate work and gone on to business school for another year and a half of specialized study, it still takes many years of training to understand what to look for and what to avoid when investing. Reading a book such as this one or Warren Buffett's annual shareholder letters is just the beginning of the thousands of hours of work and study required to become competent.

People ask why I don't conduct seminars on investing and financial planning like Suze Orman, Dave Ramsey, and other self-proclaimed financial gurus. People want to come by twice a year and have me teach them what I know. It's crazy to think that. Don't listen to people who say they can teach you to invest with a seminar or two. Don't listen to people who want to sell you their online investing programs.

When you have a situation that requires legal expertise, hire an attorney and pay their fee. You're going to get the proper documents for your specific state, containing the specific information (and protection) that you need. Whether it's closing on your house or reviewing an important agreement for your business, have an attorney review all the documents. There are lots of so-called experts out there telling you to save a couple of bucks. I think it's a grave mistake, just as I think it's a mistake to build your own patio.

Divorce is another challenge you should always rely on an attorney to help you through. There's a professor of behavioral finance who said everyone should go through a divorce because it's a tremendous learning experience. Having gone through divorce, I can't say I'd recommend the experience because it can be incredibly traumatic. However, sometimes it's likely better that two people break up for the kids' sake, as well as their own. Though I feel like I'm better able to help people going through a divorce due to my experience, I still recommend that you retain an attorney. There are so many details that a professional attorney can bring up that you might not think of, especially during a time of emotional turmoil when it's difficult to think clearly. Many times, there are unique circumstances that require specific knowledge to uncover before the paperwork is signed. People are sometimes too anxious just to get the whole process over with and later discover there were issues that were never discussed because no one knew to bring them up. They're willing to sign a document just to get it done.

Having gone through the experience of a divorce, and been a single dad with three kids, I believe there are a lot of little things that are often missed, usually things having to do with the kids. You really want to think about that document before you sign it; think about every contingency, every scenario you can imagine that might create a problem and make sure it's addressed in the separation agreement. Having an attorney to help work through these contingencies is vital. Even they won't be able to help cover every possibility, but they may be able to help you avoid arguments about who will host your child's birthday party and work out visitation hours during holidays. It's critical to have an attorney who has written thousands of divorce agreements walk you through yours.

About Trusts

There is a good deal of misinformation regarding the use of trusts, much of it propelled by self-proclaimed financial gurus hawking their lucrative legal services. Contrary to their recommendations, everyone does not need a trust. That was true before the passage of the 2017 *Tax Cuts and Jobs Act,* and it's true for even more people now.

When one of these TV trust promoters tells you it's an easy, inexpensive process, change the channel. Their advice to fill out their simple form, file it with your county clerk and you're good to go is a marketing ploy that can leave you with a false sense of confidence. In my opinion, you would be better served seeking the counsel of an attorney who's been practicing estate law for 20 or 30 years and is familiar with your state's laws to secure a proper will and other related documents. It may cost you $1,000 or more but you can relax knowing you're receiving experienced advice and guidance. If you are part of the overwhelming majority, after evaluating your circumstances, a reputable, experienced attorney may tell you there's no need for a trust unless you desire particular protections.

In my experience, there are primarily three reasons why you should consider a trust:

➢ Reduce Estate Taxes
➢ Privacy
➢ Strings from the Grave

Estate Tax

Individuals can still gift up to $15,000 annually to as many people as they like (even the mail man) without incurring a gift tax or filing. Married couples can gift $30,000. Anything in excess of these amounts reduces your federal estate tax exemption. Tuition and medical payments above the excluded amount can be made.

The *Tax Cuts and Jobs* Act resulted in a roughly $11.2 million estate tax exemption for individuals in 2018, and, as it's indexed for inflation, the amount should rise annually. Married couples now receive a roughly $22.4 million exemption. The law's sunset means that, absent further Congressional action, the exemption amount would revert to the $5 million base, indexed.[64]

This means far fewer estates will be subject to the levy—the Joint Committee on Taxation estimates the number of taxable estates will drop from 5,000 to 1,800 under the new law in 2018. By comparison, 52,000 estates paid the tax in 2000 when the exemption was $675,000.

Obviously, the estates of the vast majority of people fall below the new threshold and so have no need of a trust to avoid estate taxes. However, individual states have differing exemption amounts that may not align with the federal amount so consulting with an attorney in your state is prudent. In addition, some states also have onerous probate fees, and as such, you may desire to setup a trust.

Privacy

Titling your assets in a trust avoids probate. For some, avoiding probate for privacy reasons is important. Proceeds from a life insurance policy and assets held in a retirement account such as a 401k or IRA bypass probate through the use of beneficiary designations. A Transfer on Death (TOD) account lets owners name beneficiaries for their stocks, bonds, and other assets without going through probate.

It's not difficult to create unintended consequences. I've seen numerous instances where couples practice their own estate planning by making their child joint owner of a vacation home or other property. That's a mistake. First, the action could be deemed a gift thereby triggering tax issues; second, it creates a potential liability issue. If the child is involved in an accident or worse, kills someone in an accident, the plaintiff's attorney can go after assets held in joint tenancy. Heirs also relinquish a portion of the step-up basis on assets owned jointly with their parent.

Step-up is the readjustment of the value of an appreciated asset for tax purposes upon inheritance. The asset receives a step-up in basis so that the beneficiary's capital gains are minimized.[65]

Better to keep assets in your name until death, then pass the assets to your designated family members. Meet with an attorney to make sure all of your assets which bypass probate are properly structured and in conformity with your will and overall estate plan.

Strings from the Grave

This humorous description refers to people who try to maintain control of assets after death. These are specific instructions to the trustee regarding distributions and other trust provisions. For example, the testator may not particularly care for his daughter's husband and not want him to get half the money from the inheritance should the couple divorce. The testator might not trust a son or daughter with money because of an alcohol or drug issue, or simply because the child hasn't displayed a responsible attitude towards money. There may be provisions required for a special needs child. There may be multiple children involved with a variety of needs, responsibilities, and financial competence. The testator may not wish to treat them equally but recognizes that doing so calls for unique instructions to the trustee.

Regardless of what you do, you can't control everything and there is no "perfect" estate plan.

The great irony about trusts is that many people who create trusts do not fund them; that is, they paid to have an attorney create the legal structure but haven't moved any assets into their trusts. One excuse is that their attorney wanted to charge them an additional fee to move their assets into the trust so they postponed. Some had intentions to do so but delayed and forgot.

For our clients in this circumstance, we move their stocks, bonds, and other investment assets into their trust account. For most, there's no tax savings because of the increased exemption but they achieve what they intended when they decided to create their trust.

In the case of an irrevocable trust, the testator loses some control in that the trust can't be amended, modified, changed, or revoked. In other words, the written terms of the trust agreement are set in stone after the trust has been created.

You can't take the property back after you transfer ownership into an irrevocable trust, so it's safe from creditors and anyone who holds a judgment against you if you want to ensure that it's preserved for your beneficiaries. You no longer own it, your trust does.[66]

Testamentary trusts are irrevocable because they're not created and funded until after their creator's death. A trustmaker can amend his will, taking out the provisions for a testamentary trust, at any point during his lifetime. It can effectively be revoked before it ever exists.[67]

A revocable trust can be dissolved or amended any time you choose provided you're still mentally competent, but these trusts don't protect against lawsuit liability or estate taxes the way irrevocable trusts do. By its very nature, you can reclaim the property you place into it at any time. The law, therefore, considers that you still own this property, so its value can be counted for purposes of qualifying for certain government benefits as well. A revocable trust automatically becomes irrevocable at your death because you're no longer available to change it or revoke it.[68]

Testamentary discretionary trusts allow the trustee a measure of control over the distributions and benefits can be conferred in a tax efficient manner.

As you can see, despite what Suze Orman and others like her who peddle trusts contend, there's nothing easy or simple about the subject of estate planning. There are myriad complexities and a host of thoughtful decisions to be made. A $150 template is grossly inadequate to address all the necessary considerations. If you don't have concerns regarding estate tax, privacy, or strings from the grave, you may not need a trust in the first place. However, it is imperative you consult with an attorney to assist with developing your will and overall estate plan.

A Fox Guarding the Henhouse

There is another danger with attendant unintended consequences involving the naming of a trustee for your estate. You want to avoid letting the fox guard the henhouse. In this case, the "fox" is the bank hired to handle both trust services and investment management of your estate. You want to avoid doing this because it takes a virtual act of God for your beneficiaries to extract themselves from that arrangement should they become in any way dissatisfied with the way the bank is administering the trust and/or managing their money.

The bank, meanwhile, can charge whatever they deem customary for the services; if the beneficiaries feel the cost is unreasonable, there isn't much they can do about it.

Take the case of Frank who has four children, two by each of two marriages. Frank wants to leave his kids an equal amount, each receiving half when they reach age 35, the balance when they turn 45. But, Frank also wants to ensure the children have access to some of the funds sooner should their circumstances dictate. He doesn't know what will happen in the years after his death, but he wants to provide some flexibility for his trustee. That's extremely hard to do if he designates a bank as trustee. There's no way some banker assigned to administer the funds can know Frank's children on a personal basis nor make a sound judgment about whether one of them is experiencing a situation wherein Frank would have wanted the child to have an early distribution if he were still alive.

The logical solution for Frank is to name his best (and willing) friend Joe as *co-trustee of his estate*, along with an *independent* trust services company. He doesn't want Joe to be saddled with the administrative tasks associated with the trust, such as filing taxes, and he knows Joe lacks the experience (and inclination) to manage the trust investments. As co-trustee, Joe can choose who will manage the investments, retaining the flexibility to change investment managers if he is dissatisfied. Ditto if he doesn't like the way the trust company is administering the trust.

Joe knows Frank's kids well, and has a good idea of what Frank would do if his youngest son, a lad who inherited Frank's entrepreneurial spirit, requests a loan prior to age 35 to start a business, or if Frank's older daughter decides to stay in school and pursue an MBA. In short, Joe is a much better arbiter of what is best for Frank's kids as the years go by than a cold, impartial banker who is a stranger to Frank's kids and knows little about their proclivities or talents beyond what is specified in Frank's will.

Employing both an independent trust company and a separate investment manager may be a little more expensive, as each will charge a fee for their services, but it's money well spent if a trust is involved. However, if there's no reason for strings from the grave, trusts likely aren't needed. Just leave the money to your heirs if you're not concerned about their ability to make sound financial decisions. If you have no concerns or entanglements, skip the trust and merely create a will. It's simpler and less expensive.

Talk About Money

Some people are uncomfortable talking about money and the future with their family, but I believe these are important conversations. Once your will has been written, it's equally important to monitor the provisions for ongoing changes and beneficiary updates for life insurance, IRA, trust, and TOD accounts. It's not uncommon to hear of someone passing and unintentionally leaving his assets to an ex-spouse because he forgot to update his will after marrying his second wife. I know of one man who left a sizeable portion of his estate—whether intentionally or accidentally—to his ex-mistress, a woman his wife knew nothing about.

Talk to your family about your intentions regarding special items. If there's a special piece of jewelry intended to go to a granddaughter, make sure that intention is known. I regularly hear stories of heirs who get into the deceased's house first, grabbing whatever they want. For illiquid property like undeveloped land or a farm, you may want to consider insurance to pay the estate tax (if necessary) and/or to ensure that heirs who don't wish to own a portion of the farm may be paid by those who want to continue in the business without being forced to liquidate. Don't make the mistake of Pablo Picasso, who died at age 91 with an estate estimated to be worth between $100 and $250 million ($1.3 billion in todays' dollars) and without a will.

The lack of a will meant that suddenly everyone in his personal life was vying for a piece of the Picasso pie. He had four children by three different women, but only one of the women was his wife. One of his mistresses, a fellow artist, had not had any children with him, but she had been with him for decades and had a well-documented influence on his work. Adding to the turmoil was the presumption that he was not the best of fathers. He was alleged to have abused one son, and ignored the two children he fathered with one of his mistresses. In short, dividing his estate was a huge disaster.[69]

If you love your children, put an estate plan in place...unless you prefer to leave chaos.

You will have a will, whether you create one or not. If you don't, a state administrator will mandate a will for you and split up your assets in a way you might not like. I know of a widow that had to go down to the county clerk's office regularly to justify the money she spent on her two children because the husband passed without a will and the couple owned their home individually rather than jointly. Under that state's law, the two small children owned half of their home and other assets, thereby complicating her financial affairs for more than a decade after his death.

I get agitated when I hear Suze Orman make trusts sound so uncomplicated, making hard and fast statements that assume the world is always black and white. It's not; it's usually one of several shades of gray, and if you ask ten attorneys for their opinion of someone's circumstances, you're likely to get ten different opinions. I suggest you ask your trusted financial advisor to recommend a local attorney with significant estate planning experience to help map a plan to meet your specific needs.

CHAPTER SIXTEEN

A Contrarian Mindset

Investing Like an Aardvark

Just as the aardvark takes an unorthodox approach to finding food, I take a contrarian approach to investing. To be a contrarian investor, you have to be willing to go against the grain and buy companies others hate. If you can buy good companies when their values have gone down, then take gains when they rebound, you have the opportunity to outperform not only the market but the stock returns of those companies.

As I previously mentioned, I'm seemingly in the only business where something selling at a significant discount doesn't get buyers excited. People shopping at Nordstrom see a suit or dress offered at 25% off and they snap up the perceived bargain, but when Proctor & Gamble is selling at 25% off, frightened stockholders can't wait to unload their shares. It's an emotional reaction that makes no sense from an investment perspective.

In the few years after founding Altrius, I believed valuations were high for the market and that investors would likely achieve lower returns than they expected. I wanted to create a money management firm that eliminated a needless expense for investors — the middle man. I desired to provide investors with a reduced-expense alternative to wealth management firms who outsource investment management (via ETFs, mutual funds or separate accounts) by giving them direct access to professional money management. Doing so eliminates the layers of fees associated with money management expenses charged in addition to the fees charged by wealth management firms and advisors.

Today, two decades later, money management fees have compressed and many inexpensive passive strategies exist through ETFs. The fee compression has been a good thing for investors, but typical all-in fees for financial planning and asset management fees charged by wealth management firms generally cost between 1.5 – 2.0% annually. By allowing investors to come directly to Altrius, we maintain a cost advantage from a pricing standpoint against our wealth management competitors while also being fully transparent with our fees and the securities we own for our clients.

Wall Street analysts and portfolio managers are often far removed from the people for whom they are investing. Growing up as a broker's son, I saw the extensive contact my dad had with his clients and realized these were not just clients but personal relationships. My dad passed away fourteen years ago but I still work with a handful of his clients, maintaining that intergenerational relationship. That's a different type of business approach than exists with most of my Wall Street friends, who are good people and smart but who rarely meet their investor clients face to face. I never forget the personal responsibility I have to my clients. I don't take that lightly, which is why I don't sleep very much. To me, the most important benchmark is the long-term success of my clients.

Eating What We Cook

I think clients find it reassuring when I show them that I own the same stocks and bonds that they do. Many financial advisors do not eat what they cook in that they do not own the same investments as their clients. Some sell their clients annuities and other high commission products. I have frequently asked other advisors if they have their own personal funds invested in the same annuities they sell their clients. In 20+ years, I've never received a positive response. My question then is, if it's good enough for your clients, why don't you own it? The answer, of course, is that the advisors don't own the same investment because it's not a good product and the fees are exorbitant.

Eating what we cook is one of the ways I align the interests of our clients with those of our firm. At Altrius, we invest our company's retirement plan assets side by side with our clients, owning the same stocks and bonds that our clients do.

Altrius works at the pleasure of our clients and just as our fee is negatively impacted if client portfolios decline during a market turndown, so too is our retirement savings. That said, we are patient long-term investors and don't make rash decisions when investing by moving in and out of stocks rapidly or changing course due to short-term news events. I take the same long-term approach in managing my business, which I hope to do for many decades to come, attempting to make the best decisions for our clients and firm over a longtime frame rather than chasing short-term gains.

Investing alongside our clients obviously displays our strong belief in our analysis and research. We design our portfolio to be sufficiently diversified to mitigate risk, but adequately concentrated to potentially outperform. We are patient investors and view every security we purchase as if we were buying a piece of a business — not simply a stock certificate. Many Wall Street analysts focus exclusively on growth. In contrast, we invest in companies with sound cash flow, global growth potential, discounted valuations and steadily growing dividends, which has enabled our clients' retirement income to grow and keep ahead of inflation over time.

Essential Traits for a Portfolio Manager

One of the most important traits for an investment analyst and portfolio manager is *humility*. Managing risk is a critical aspect of what I do, and every morning I wake up and question where I might be wrong, whether it's about companies I've purchased, the current asset allocation I've set, my economic outlook or market strategy.

It's impossible to manage a portfolio without occasionally making mistakes. Learning from those mistakes is what helps keep me humble. As a pilot, overconfidence can lead you to take risks with the airplane that you shouldn't. Young pilots are especially susceptible, believing they are bulletproof. I've lost a lot of friends who flew airplanes.

Overconfidence can kill, whether it's flying an airplane or managing a portfolio. Humility teaches you the importance of not having to swing at every pitch, living to fight another day, and thinking about where you might be wrong. Humility helps you avoid overconfidence that can blow up your portfolio. It's in short supply on Wall Street, which is populated with overconfident young Ivy League graduates who think they're smarter than the market. They have the idea that they are going to become the next wealthy Wall Street titan. They lack humility and can't imagine being wrong about their ideas. They make horrible mistakes, such as using leverage with huge concentrated positions, and they blow themselves — and their clients — up.

I made a mistake with Mattel. I first bought the stock in 2007, during the lead paint scare in China. It seemed to be a good entry point to invest in the company as the stock price had declined almost 30% initially. I began adding to the position as the stock was declining.

Part of our smart beta strategy is to maintain equal weighting of our individual positions at approximately 1% of the portfolio. This helps prevent volatility in any single issue from jeopardizing the entire portfolio. When the stock price of an issue declines, our weighting drops and we add more shares, unless my thesis on the company has changed. For example, if the stock goes down 20%, our weighting drops from 1% to .8%, so we buy more shares, which brings the allocation back up to around 1%.

When the price of Mattel stock recovered, I looked really smart. Our weighting had gone up to 1.4% in 2011 so we began selling shares, taking profits and bringing our allocation back down closer to 1%. At this point, the stock was soaring and got a bit costly, selling at 22-24 times earnings, but the dividend yield was still at about 5%. As I've discussed, I use a three-pronged approach: value, dividends, and global growth generation. I'm constantly looking for higher than average dividends, a reasonable P/E ratio, and global growth generation.

The stock continued to run up and while the dividend was still attractive, the valuation wasn't and I should have sold it — but I didn't. Sometimes, I will hold on to an issue even though it has risen in price to the point where, technically, it no longer qualifies as a value stock because I hate to give up the healthy dividend yield, have clients pay taxes on the gains, while also believing that growth managers may drive the company's price even higher since its cash flow and earnings growth remain strong. It's typically at this point when the analysts come out with a "strong buy" recommendation and the growth/momentum managers jump in and start buying. This is what occurred in 2011 and again in 2015 with Mattel.

I took gains at this point, shedding some of the shares. In retrospect, I should have liquidated all of it. That was a mistake. Mattel lost their exclusive rights to sell dolls appearing in Disney movies and the stock plummeted. Taking a long-term approach, we started buying Mattel again after it took a huge hit, sticking to my thesis that toys aren't dead though children are certainly playing with electronic toys more often. Mattel is an example of why you have to stay humble. These distressed companies can be extremely volatile.

I believe in the long-term thesis that supported my decision, but like every investment, I'm constantly reevaluating my decisions, questioning whether I might be missing something. This is what makes investing so difficult. There is never a big green light that says invest, or a big red light that says avoid this. Though many investors want to believe there is a sure-fire formula for success – and charlatans shilling such programs will always sell such trading systems – there simply isn't a magic formula. There is always uncertainty to deal with.

Keep in mind that as a value investor and contrarian, you can alternately look really smart or awfully dumb for both short and longer periods of time. You're the aardvark going against the grain, out hunting ants at midnight and sometimes your hard work may not be rewarded for some time. You might enjoy a belly full of ants for dinner, or a storm could come up and you get soaked and go home hungry.

The other important trait for portfolio managers is *sticktuitiveness*, the concept of sticking with your thesis unless the world has changed and children aren't playing with toys any more. If you're dealing with horses and buggies or Polaroid cameras, you have to be willing to say that you've made a mistake. A lot of areas are gray, however. Everyone now emails but do people still go to the post office and mail letters and packages? Yes. What about newspapers or telephone landlines? Do people still read local newspapers? My thesis is yes, because they want to see the local obituaries, the results of their kid's sports team or other local news. Newspapers aren't completely dead yet. There's that puff of smoke left in the cigarette butt that was thrown away. As for telephones, our children may never have a landline because of mobile phones and the internet but some people still want a landline for security in case their cell phone coverage quits.

I lend money (owning the bond rather than the stock) to companies that may possibly be in a dying business, and yes, their industry might completely evaporate at some point, but I don't expect they will go bankrupt during the next few years. With paper-thin margins, the grocery business may be extinguished by Amazon at some point and I don't want to own their stocks, but lending them money over the next few years may prove to be a good investment for us.

The other crucial trait is *intellectual curiosity*. In my opinion, a portfolio manager should always be intellectually curious, constantly wanting to learn, to find different ideas and unique investment opportunities. Unfortunately, I think a lot of otherwise intellectually curious managers lack humility to the point of stubbornness. That can be dangerous when someone refuses to acknowledge that they might be wrong. On the other hand, when you've done your homework and are convinced you are making the right choice, you must have the courage to stick to your convictions, particularly as a contrarian investor, even when the rest of the world says you're wrong.

The horror of this is that you can feel like an idiot for a few years, which will seem like an eternity. We're living in a McDonald's society where people want instant gratification; it can be arduous to let your thesis play out over two or three years. Few people have the patience to wait a month, much less years. It takes genuine mettle to hang in there with your investments. Lots of managers have the intellectual capacity but lack the guts to stick it out. If they're working for a Wall Street firm, chances are they'll be fired before their decisions can play out. If their investment style falls out of favor, they can be gone in a flash, just because they made the wrong pick in the short term. Had their bosses had the foresight to let their thesis play out over three years, the people they fired might have looked pretty smart.

Wall Street has a turnover mentality with instant gratification. It wants quarter by quarter profit. I believe it's wiser to keep your eye on the big picture.

What Constitutes Diversification?

Consider stocks within a portfolio as if they were pencils. From a risk management standpoint, it's a lot easier to break a single pencil than it is to break 75 pencils. A broadly diversified portfolio containing 75 stocks has a much better chance of success than a portfolio containing just a few stocks. The same holds true for bond portfolios.

There are so many instances of money managers who blew up their mutual funds by putting large percentages of their investors' money into just a few stocks. TV's Jim Cramer has been heard to tell his audience that they can be adequately diversified if they own four stocks: an industrial, a financial, a utility, and another stock. That's not true diversification; you can't be sufficiently diversified with just a handful of stocks. Many economic studies have suggested that the "right" number to achieve diversification is somewhere between 30 and 40 stocks while others have suggested 60 to as many as 100 as a better number.

Currently, our portfolio contains roughly 75 U.S. and international stocks. There's no "right" number but it's certainly not four stocks as Cramer has suggested in his "Am I Diversified?" segment on his show "Mad Money".

Penny Stocks and Common Sense

As mentioned, a $10,000 stock can be cheap and a $1 stock can be expensive. There's no shortage of investors willing to buy penny stocks. If I asked you to invest in my company even though we're going to lose a couple million this year and maybe three million next year, but hey, we're getting lots of clicks on our website and our new marketing campaign is about to kick off. We're sure to turn things around over the next 5-6 years and we have the potential to be hugely profitable after that. So, do you want to invest with me?

A prudent investor would, of course, not throw her money out the window. She would recognize that the company was a penny stock, losing money every year and that making a gain on such a speculative investment entails hoping some suckers come in and boost the price of the stock so that she isn't the last person holding the bag.

People invest in this kind of hope. There are hundreds of newsletters touting this stuff. Please understand that this is rampant speculation and not investing. In my opinion, you would be as poorly served placing a bet on black (or red) on a roulette wheel in Las Vegas as you would be speculating in the tomfoolery of penny stocks.

Fallacy of the Financial Fast Track

Investors are continuously bombarded by discount brokerage commercials urging them to trade, trade, trade. They're exhortations are understandable; getting people to trade is how discount brokers generate income. But what's good for them is not necessarily good for their investor clients, despite their claims that they can teach people how to trade effectively.

One commercial floats the idea of a financial coach who can teach you how to trade, drawing a tenuous parallel of a coach teaching someone how to shoot a basketball. Think of how absurd that idea is. I have had people ask me if I can teach them how to invest the way I do. Sure; no problem. Just start by reading these five or six books on the fundamentals of dividend stocks and value investing; then go back to school and acquire an MBA with a concentration in Finance; then come study under me for a few years and learn my process. If you work for 50 hours a week for three years, I might be able to get you to where you're modestly competent to work at Altrius.

I wasn't a good pilot until I flew for many years. I wasn't a really good money manager until I did it for about a decade. Reaching that level assumes you're willing to put in 100 hours a week, which means there isn't much time for anything else. If you're only working a normal 40 hour work week, it could take you two decades to get really good at something. It's ridiculous to imagine that someone can become adept at investing by attending a couple of seminars or from a few hours of coaching. In his book, *Outliers*, Malcolm Gladwell makes a great argument using the "10,000-hour Rule", which asserts that the key to achieving world-class expertise in anything is to practice correctly for 10,000 hours.

Yet people continue to look for the fast track to riches, believing there must be a short cut to investment success. I had an investor ask me to read some loony idea he got from Porter Stansberry, the "End of America" doomsday fanatic who takes an economic principle and distorts it to the point of absurdity. I asked him if he realized that the SEC brought a case against Stansberry for disseminating false information and that he and his company had been fined and were ordered by a U.S. District Court to pay $1.5 million in restitution and civil penalties?[70] "Yeah, but I think some of his stuff is good," the investor insisted. It may be true that there's a sucker born every minute.

Another investor asked if I could send some information to their son, who wants to day trade. I said no. Tell him to study and acquire a CFA or go to a reputable business school and then maybe get into the industry. For the love of God, do not let him day trade. Worst case, let him lose money now, while he's young and doesn't know what he's doing. Let him learn that you can't get rich quick.

None of my clients have become wealthy by some get rich scheme. In 20+ years of doing this, I've never seen a person become wealthy overnight; they become wealthy by slowly and painstakingly saving over time, or by building a business and working hard for 20 or 30 years. Nobody becomes wealthy overnight unless they win the lottery. Certainly, nobody has become wealthy reading Porter Stansbury's investment newsletter. You become wealthy over time, working hard and remaining disciplined to get there.

It is frustrating to me listening to people who think there is some clandestine investment formula. It doesn't exist but that doesn't stop people from searching for it. All the schemes that purport to have the secret have been debunked. Even if you believe such a formula exists, there's a computer program that will execute it faster than you can. If it existed, there would be a hedge fund quant managing it and he would have virtually all the investment money in the world under management because everyone would be using his system — that he would most certainly refuse to divulge.

I used to wonder how some of the insane investing gobbledygook ever got anyone to part with their money, but no longer. It seems the wackier the concept, the more it appeals to people looking for investing's secret formula.

Don't listen to the peddlers telling you they have the secret. If they did, why would they share the information? Ignore the brokers telling you how to make a fortune day trading. Trading is hazardous to your wealth. Don't confuse these salespeople with fiduciaries who are obliged to put your interests first.

Gold and Gold Coins

Historically, an ounce of gold has equated to the price of a nice men's suit. Gold, currently at $1,200, will today still buy you a quality suit unless you desire a more expensive Italian import or shop for a Canali on eBay like I do, where you can find them for about half that price. A century ago, an ounce of gold was worth about $20, the approximate cost of a durable man's suit in 1920.

Gold is a commodity. Its price mimics inflation over time though fluctuating widely in the short term based upon speculation. When the Fed raised interest rates to stifle inflation in the early 1980s, gold dropped from over $600 to almost

$300, contrary to the ubiquitous commercials that claim gold will always retain its value.

If you think inflation is going to rise, gold can be a hedge, but I believe we are in a prolonged period of low inflation due to technological productivity gains and globalization. If you decide to buy gold as a hedge against inflation, I suggest a futures contract or an ETF. What you want to avoid are gold coins because there are a host of people in the middle of these transactions. First, there are the miners who get the gold out of the ground; then the people who clean it and make it shiny; then there are the people who mint and protect it, followed by the brokers who sponsor all those commercials. You have to pay their commissions, both when you buy coins and again when you want to sell them. Of course, you need to store the coins somewhere, so you either buy a safe for your house or pay an intermediary for storage.

Never buy gold coins, unless you think the Russians are going to attack and that flipping them a few coins is going to do you some good. If you want to own gold, buy the ETF (GLD or IAU) and hold it in your custodian account. Some people — like the preppers — get a sense of security from owning gold, the same way some feel more secure with a wad of cash in their drawer.

Aside from the preppers, there are the people with a lot of money who hoard gold and keep it somewhere close to their private jet in case they need to slip off to some protected island. These are usually people involved in some nefarious activity or dictators of a third world nation.

I concur with Warren Buffet's appraisal of the value of gold when he says, "You could take all the gold that's ever been mined and it would fill a cube 67 feet in each direction. For what that's worth at current gold prices, you could buy all — not some — of the farmland in the United States, plus, you could buy 10 Exxon Mobil's, plus have $1 trillion of walking-around money. Or you could have a big cube of metal. Which would you take? Which is going to produce more value?"

Some people enjoy gold as an adornment. The ring on my finger has a great emotional value for me, but has zero utility and is worth maybe $50 at a pawn shop. My wedding band for which I paid $100 hasn't appreciated a cent since our vows. Gold doesn't produce anything, pay a dividend or create any jobs, outside of its own mining industry. Its intrinsic value is its beauty, like flowers, but it has no tangible utility the way a company does. I'd prefer to own a company with growth potential, not something that hangs around my neck or sits in a bureau drawer.

A comparable folly is our fascination with diamonds. Where is the value in a diamond? It's simply a shiny rock but for hundreds of years, it's been valued for its presumed rarity and people are willing to pay outrageous prices for it. I can buy a piece of glass that looks just as pretty. Diamonds are able to cut things well and that's about the extent of their usefulness, other than possibly making some people happy for a couple of weeks due to its sparkling nature.

> *"Gold gets dug out of the ground in Africa, or someplace. Then we melt it down, dig another hole, bury it again and pay people to stand around guarding it. It has no utility. Anyone watching from Mars would be scratching their head."*
> Warren Buffett

Confusion Among the Giants

In the noisy financial services sector, it's difficult to tell the difference between a broker working for a large bank, a financial services representative at your local bank, an insurance agent pitching financial advice via annuities or life insurance, online brokerage firms offering advice on a green sofa, robo-advisors with model ETF platforms, and accounting firms selling mutual funds. Some firms offer an important difference: Registered Investment Advisors that provide wealth management services as a fiduciary for a fee without commissions, thereby limiting many conflicts of interest.

Altrius is such a firm, acting as a fiduciary to our clients. In addition to providing wealth management services, we also act as a money manager providing separately managed accounts and sub-advising a mutual fund for financial advisors around the country. Most financial advisors, brokers, agents, and representatives outsource money management to firms such as ours, thereby adding layers of cost. In contrast, Altrius does not outsource money management functions to other firms, instead purchasing individual stocks and bonds for our clients through our proprietary income-focused process.

There are some very large money managers able to buy a lot of commercial time on television. They have an obvious marketing advantage over firms like us when it comes to maintaining a high profile, thanks to their massive advertising budgets. Some of them are what I refer to as noble competitors in that, like us, they are fiduciaries charging fees rather than commissions and are legally bound to put the interests of clients first. Unlike Altrius however, only a very few of these noble RIA fiduciaries claim compliance with the Global Investment Performance Standards (GIPS ®). GIPS verification is an independent third party review of an investment management firm's performance processes and procedures.

Though some firms are both fee-only Registered Investment Advisors, and GIPS verified money managers, that's typically where the similarities end, as our investment processes are significantly different. Many managers lean towards growth versus our focus on value and dividends. There are some other significant differences where I believe we add value.

Though some large firms manage individual stocks like us, most are simply too large to manage a portfolio of smaller capitalization bonds: instead, they utilize ETFs and large capitalization bonds. Our smaller size is an advantage. Being smaller, we can own the types of bonds larger institutions cannot, due to their size, as they would effectively own a great majority of a company's debt. In contrast, we are able to provide a customized portfolio of 60 – 100 individual bonds producing above average income to our clients. In addition, our fixed income portfolio usually provides a significantly higher yield while maintaining a shorter duration and maturity to potentially better protect against rising interest rates.

Altrius has always had a value-driven approach whereas many money managers lean towards a growth/momentum strategy. It's common to find money managers' portfolios laden with growth stocks like Amazon and Google (Alphabet) — both with very expensive multiples.

Though I am a customer of both companies, I think buying a company at 100 times earnings is crazy and though I have no intention of ever selling my company, should someone offer me 100 times earnings due to our potential growth opportunities, I would be foolish not to accept!

Growth/momentum strategies have been driven greatly by FANG (Facebook, Amazon, Netflix, and Google) stocks and are currently highly appreciated and expensive. In contrast, value stocks have not been driven to excessive valuations. Over the long term, a value investment approach has meaningfully outperformed a strategy of buying expensive (high-multiple) stocks. However, cycles persist. Value investing has had several periods of significant underperformance. The inability of most investors to stick with a value approach during such cyclical reversals is likely what enables the "value premium" to persist over the long term. Moreover, the short-term, performance-chasing tendencies of most investors pushes the pendulum still further.

While it's possible that growth's outperformance may continue over the next decade, I believe the greatest benefit of our value approach is that our clients don't have to "hope" for growth. With a growth/momentum strategy, you must hope your manager can outperform, enabling him to sell stocks at appreciated levels in order to provide you with retirement income. In contrast, should our portfolio decline in value (which is inevitable during recessions in both portfolio management styles), the basket of stocks we own will potentially provide 3 ½% to 4% in dividends, which enables our clients to "get paid to wait" for the price appreciation we expect over longer periods of time.

I believe our three-pronged approach of dividends, value, and global growth generation is a more prudent manner to manage assets than a growth/momentum strategy. Though extremely competitive, I honestly don't care whether I outperform other leading managers over the next decade as I believe strongly that our approach provides a greater certainty of retirement success for our clients.

It's a David and Goliath challenge, but one I welcome.

What Defines a "Legendary" Investor?

The adjective "legendary" is commonly used to describe some people in our industry, principally portfolio managers and analysts. My dictionary defines legendary as "remarkable enough to be famous." A number of managers (or their advertising agencies) have anointed themselves legendary but when I compare their long-term investing records against ours and broad market indices, I find they come up short — in some cases, far short.

One of my firm's advisors said his definition of a legendary investor is someone who has made a really good market call, but given the industry's talking heads on TV are daily making predictions about the markets, it's inevitable that they will be right occasionally. So, if an analyst calls for a 30% drop in the Dow every week for three years and it finally happens, does that make him a financial luminary? I don't think so.

There's virtually no drawback to making bold predictions because no one is ever held accountable for their miscalculations. Remember the Wall Street sell-side analyst I previously referred to who predicted a $200 a barrel "super spike" for oil?" He's worth millions today but I wonder how many investors lost their shirts following his disastrous call?

In the summer of 2008, I got out of commodities completely. It was one of those wonderfully rare times when my timing was nearly perfect. We had already experienced remarkable returns in our commodity positions and, I believed demand was outstripping supply significantly while speculation was the primary cause of higher prices. Of course, oil plummeted during the financial crisis bringing prices back to reasonable levels.

During my 20-year plus career, I've made several sound investment decisions (based on valuation, not timing) with major financial implications for our clients. In addition to the aforementioned commodities sale, our clients weren't decimated during the 2000 tech bubble implosion as I wouldn't purchase high flying tech and dot.com stocks which didn't pay dividends and were selling at astronomical valuations. In the latter part of the decade, when Microsoft, Cisco, and Intel began paying dividends and sold for reasonable valuations, I snapped them up and the companies were long-term holdings for us.

Admittedly, the calls didn't always come with perfect timing, but that's not a realistic goal in any case. I got out of Real Estate Investment Trusts (REITs) in 2005 when many were just beginning to jump on the real estate band wagon and websites popped up touting real estate with monikers such as "Bubbles are for Bath Tubs." Driven by the mania, REIT ETFs like the iShares U.S. Real Estate (IYR) continued to go up another 30+%, but the crash of 2008-2009 cost a lot of investors 50% or more. It took over a decade for the iShares U.S. Real Estate ETF to recover its losses.

Though health care stocks are generally identified in the value category, I was fortunately underweight the sector for many years due to valuation. Displaying little growth in the years before the passage of Obamacare in 2010, the sector sold off further. I took a very contrarian position, purchasing many health care companies I believed were undervalued while common Wall Street thinking hypothesized that Obamacare would crush health care companies.

The same was true for the defense sector. After Obama was elected President, many on Wall Street believed that his administration would decrease defense spending. I, however, didn't believe the world was any safer. With defense contractors selling at very low valuations and paying exceptionally attractive dividends, I began moving into Lockheed Martin, Northrop Grumman, and Raytheon in 2011 and 2012. This contrarian approach led to exceptional returns for our clients and investors.

On December 19, 2010 during a *60 Minutes* interview, financial analyst Meredith Whitney stated "there's not a doubt in my mind that you will see a spate of municipal bond defaults. You could see 50 sizable defaults, 50 to 100 sizable defaults, more. This will amount to hundreds of billions of dollars' worth of defaults" and, "it'll be something to worry about within the next 12 months."[71]

During her interview, I had two strong thoughts: First, that we were going to receive a lot of worried calls from clients Monday morning (which we did); and second, that this was going to be a wonderful opportunity to buy municipal bonds at attractive valuations. I did so, of course, as billions of dollars left the municipal bond market in the panic-selling during the subsequent months after Whitney's interview. After locking in attractive municipal bonds yields for our clients during that period, I haven't purchased significant positions in municipal bonds in well over six years due to low interest rates (and high prices).

As Bitcoin pushed toward 20,000, I published a blog in early January of 2018 about the lunacy of Bitcoin. Today, it's at 6,400. Will it eventually drop to zero? I don't know, but I recognized the similarities between Bitcoin, the tech bubble, and the tulip craze and warned my clients against investing when many others were recommending it.

My most recent admonition has been directed toward growth stocks in general and FANG in particular, the term coined by CNBC's *Mad Money* host Jim Cramer. I don't know if or when this one is going to blow, but I'm certainly not jumping on the crazy train. These stocks could keep flying for some time but should they revert to the mean of normalized earnings and prices, it will be ugly for investors (and advisors) knee-deep in FANG momentum stocks.

That's the idea of value investing. You don't have to swing at every pitch. You can't call every recession. There are too many people who have made great calls, but then been wrong for the rest of their careers, trying to make that next great call. As Warren Buffett has stated: "Forecasts may tell you a great deal about the forecaster; they tell you nothing about the future."

Though I've made plenty of prudent investment decisions during my career, I would never endeavor to call myself a "legendary" investor. As I mentioned humility being a trait short on Wall Street and important to one's survival and success in this difficult business, I've also made plenty of mistakes from which I've learned. I missed the energy bubble because I was unaware of the technological advancements energy companies were making. When it enabled sideways drilling via fracking, it cut the price of oil in half. Oil wasn't overpriced at $80 from a supply demand side in my opinion; however, when the technology changed, it immediately changed the world. Now we're back up at close to $70 a barrel.

I also didn't see the Great Recession related to the financial crisis of 2007-2008 and U.S. subprime mortgage collapse of 2007-2009. Though accurately predicting that real estate was overvalued in 2005, I didn't understand the extent of leverage that major Wall Street banks had, including the proliferation of levered Collateralized Debt Obligations (CDOs) being sold hand over fist by financial institutions to unsuspecting investors. Though I didn't purchase CDOs, I didn't believe stocks were terribly overvalued leading up to the collapse as earnings were being propped up through financial sales volume and economic activity was strong throughout the global economy. As such, though not suffering as great a fall as the overall market, our balanced Global Income strategy was lower by almost 25% in 2008.

I did, however, purchase many distressed bank bonds selling at over 20% yields during the crisis as I believed that the federal government had to make the decision to back the financial complex or suffer great calamity. Though this wasn't apparent to every Congressman initially, the Troubled Asset Relief Program (TARP) was eventually passed by Congress to purchase toxic assets and equity from financial institutions to strengthen the financial sector.

Fortunately for our clients, the dividends and interest payments enabled them to remain invested and not panic-sell their distressed stock and bond holdings. We eventually recovered the predominantly paper losses and none of our clients had to go back to work or change their lifestyle in the worst economic collapse since the Great Depression, a fact of which I am exceptionally proud.

On Hiring Altrius Associates

I fear there is an overpowering temptation among members of our industry to create star status for themselves. It's an addiction that has prompted me to largely avoid hiring experienced analysts at Altrius, instead recruiting bright, young recent graduates. Philosophically, I would rather hire someone right out of college or someone still in their 20's or 30's and inculcate them in the Altrius investment philosophy. I believe I'm better off hiring young people who are smarter than I am and training them in our process, values, and culture versus hiring a 40-something who has already embraced bad Wall Street habits.

I have to recruit these young people before they are drawn like moths to the bright lights of Wall Street and get zapped. So many of the young people entering the financial services industry dream of becoming the next Gordon Gecko, believing that's what Wall Street is all about: Making big bets and getting rich quick. They hear stories of overnight riches and think they have to make a name for themselves. Most get a face full of reality and learn the hard way, but luckily, they can make those mistakes when they are young and their careers have time to recover. Unfortunately, it is often the young people who are pumping the phones, advising investors about their financial futures. The consequences of their advice on trusting investors are often of little consequence to them or their brokerage firm employers. They want people to trade. Like the "legendary" analysts whose botched calls cost their clients untold millions and are rarely held accountable for their errors, those who make such gambles are not often forced to pay for their transgressions, instead walking away from their blown-up hedge funds and firms with millions while their clients and investors are left with a pittance of their savings.

A Long-Term Perspective

My clients know I don't invest based on three-month time horizons or short-term expected outcomes. To the contrary, I believe that a critical element of our investment process and edge is our discipline to maintain a longer-term (multi-year) perspective while other market participants overreact to short-term performance swings, daily news flow, and other emotional/behavioral triggers. I try to minimize the harmful impact of "myopic loss aversion" on our investment decision-making that can come from paying too much attention to short-term results.

There are *always* risks and uncertainties when investing in equities that have the potential to cause significant shorter-term price declines. Whether it is a trade war, a geopolitical event, an unexpected economic shock, a monetary policy mistake or innumerable other factors, stocks can deliver big losses in the shorter-term (one- to three-year) periods. Market corrections and bear markets happen. An investor must be able to withstand these drops, stay the course, and stick to a long-term plan — assuming it was well-designed and aligned with their financial objectives.

No one can consistently and accurately predict the timing, outcomes, and market reactions of these types of macro/geopolitical uncertainties. A corollary, therefore, is that people who try to do so are very likely to detract more value than they add over time. They're more likely to get whipsawed by the daily news headlines and changing "expert" opinions amid market ups and downs. While they may feel better in the moment of their action, they end up with a worse outcome than if they had remained disciplined in their investment approach.

I believe it is far better to stick with one's long-term strategic asset allocation, applying disciplined rebalancing, and making portfolio changes away from your strategic allocation only when you have high confidence (based on strong evidence and analysis) that you have an edge. This is possible if you understand what the market is discounting in current prices, why you think the market is wrong, and why the odds are stacked in your favor that you are likely to ultimately be proven right. Even then, of course, there is no guarantee you will be right. In fact, it is guaranteed you *won't* be right every time. That's why portfolio diversification, scenario analysis, and risk management are also critical elements.

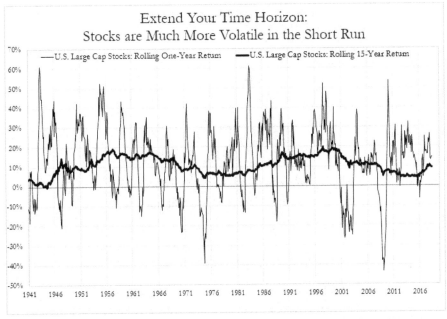

Fig. 16.1: Short Run Volatility

As mentioned earlier, one of the key elements of the edge I think Altrius has is "time arbitrage"— the willingness and ability to take a longer-term analytical view and maintain a longer-term investment horizon than other market participants. We don't have to respond to all the short-term market noise and we don't play the short-term trading (guessing) game.

Our globally diversified portfolios are positioned to potentially perform well over the long term and to be resilient across a range of potential scenarios founded upon our value-based, income-focused process among our foreign and domestic stocks and our unconstrained fixed income strategy.

"Investing should be more like watching paint dry or watching grass grow. If you want excitement, take $800 and go to Las Vegas."
Paul Samuelson, Economist

EPILOGUE

Closing Thoughts

The aardvark calmly watches other animals
chase one another under the hot sun

If I could give you only one piece of investment advice, it would be this: question everything.

Question the biases of the people selling you investment products. Question the motivations of the "experts" who endorse an investment or strategy. Who do they work for? Who pays their salary or commissions?

Wall Street will continue to manufacture financial novelties that appeal to the emotional biases of most investors. Like snake oil salesmen of the last century, they will tell you they have the magic formula you've been searching for. There will always be something new that's purportedly been back tested and "if you had bought this investment five years ago, you would now have (fill in the blanks) because it's better than anything before. They'll tout the securitization and leverage as safe when it is inherently dangerous, what Warren Buffett referred to as financial weapons of mass destruction. [72]

You must be ceaselessly skeptical and question these claims, understanding that when these "innovations" blow up, no one will take responsibility and offer to reimburse you for making the mistake of believing them. Just as no one in the financial community or government took responsibility for the financial crisis: not the banks that loaned 100% on overvalued properties to people lacking the income or documentation to buy them; not the regulators who didn't perform the required oversight; not the rating agencies who rubber stamped unrealistic valuations; and not Congress who overly deregulated and promised home ownership to everyone. They all abdicated responsibility for the meltdown and quietly moved on with their careers. The banks, brokerage firms, regulators, and politicians are all still with us, telling us what they think we want to hear and fabricating new "gee whiz" investments they think we will buy.

Beware of investments containing leverage; they are inherently dangerous. They can blow up and take their investors with them. Don't trust investments based on mathematical risk models, such as value at risk (VaR) models.[73] They are ostensibly founded on sophisticated algorithms that sound impressive but fail to take into consideration that markets are governed by human behavior, not computerized projections. When the issuers of the latest leveraged product assure the investing public that the maximum downside is 13.2%, don't believe them; it can go down 50% (or more) under the right circumstances. It has happened before and it will likely happen again. Mathematical models may offer some guidance; however, there's no way to accurately predict the future returns for any strategy, nor especially for a black swan type of event. Investment management is a 24/7 365 days-a-year obsession managing risk.

As long as there are people on Wall Street whose incomes are determined by how much product they can securitize and peddle to a guileless public, the temptation for you to join their party will be there. Don't trust Wall Street to do what's in your best interest.

I believe capitalism is the holiest of all financial isms; look at what it has done to improve our lives over the last couple of centuries compared to the thousands of years before. But capitalism is not perfect. It's a relatively new ism—a complex one—and we are still learning how to use it most beneficially for everyone. It can also be a dirty business that leads to greed. As much as I support some regulations, you can't regulate everything. You can't regulate integrity and responsibility. People do bad things for money and, as an investor, you have to be vigilant and protect yourself.

Question everything and everyone before you give them your money.

Public vs Private Investments

On the argument of public versus private investments, I come down firmly on the side of public. The private equity guys are quite smart and they make a lot of money taking companies private, then public again, sometimes multiple times throughout a company's history. They are sophisticated estimators who will place a valuation on a company before the marketplace determines an actual price. They lock their clients in for the long term and are permitted to operate without a big red light above their heads flashing a daily valuation determined by an open market.

I sometimes envy that private equity guys lock their clients in long term, but I'll stick with publicly traded investments for my clients believing it's superior. Liquidity is one reason, but also because you are able to dollar cost average on the way down when the analysts and other investors are in full retreat. If you don't need the cash flow from your dividends, you can reinvest as the stock is going down.

Even Nobel Prize Winners Get it Wrong

Harry Markowitz was awarded a Nobel Prize for his hypothesis on Modern Portfolio Theory (MPT). It suggests that it is possible to construct an "efficient frontier" of optimal portfolios, offering the maximum possible expected return for a given level of risk.[74] Markowitz believed that investing should always be passive. His ideas became the mantra for virtually every investment broker on the planet for a time: "Toss it all into a few mutual funds and let the efficient market do the rest."

There was a problem, however: the theory didn't work, not even for Markowitz's own portfolio. Years later, he admitted as much, saying that his work was mischaracterized and that markets indeed aren't efficient. That's tantamount to the Pope admitting there is no God. Suddenly, the advocates were all reassessing their efficient market positions. "Hey, maybe markets aren't efficient after all."

An irony in all of this is that the proponents of MPT, Fama, French and Markowitz, all came from the highly respected University of Chicago, and from the same school arises the concept of behavioral finance postulated by Daniel Kahneman.

In my opinion, the economists have strayed too far down the path of mathematics. Economics is a human science, one that can't be drilled down easily. It's nice that we have calculus, but we can change our minds in a second, which changes all the models. Instead of looking at economics as science, we should understand that the mind is incredibly complex and that finance is likely more art than science.

It's Behavior, not Algorithms

You need to be prepared for the unexpected and since there's no way to know in advance what that will be, you have to be patient and willing to hang in there during downhill market swings.

Whatever negative event you might contemplate happening, there's always something worse that you didn't imagine. That's one reason why the rationale behind these mathematical models is such nonsense. They are untrustworthy because they are based on algorithms rather than human behavior. You have to assess risk as it conflates with people, not computers; behavioral science, not physical science.

The next crisis is going to transpire at some point and you must continually manage risk in anticipation of that occurrence. You have to recognize that the price of a security is an illusion of its true value. The price is established by what the market forces say a security is worth, and during times of irrational exuberance, the price is going to be too high, even though most investors are willing to pay it because of their fear of missing out (FOMO), which motivates them to continue paying the inflated price until reality sets in and the price plunges. At any given time, the price of a security is not the true value of the company. It may be too high or too cheap, but it almost never represents the exact true value.

When the price is on the downside, the analysts are downgrading the stock, investors are clamoring to sell off, and the short sellers are coming on board. That's when value investors display their true contrarian grit and buy on the way down. It's always better to be too early than too late because there is so much more liquidity and volume on the way down when everyone else is selling. You must have the courage to push your way in—past all the lemmings rushing to get out—and understand that while it may seem counterintuitive, there are going to be price markdowns you can take advantage of. You must be willing to continue to buy when nobody else wants the stock, but the reward for this strategy is you continue to collect the dividends while you wait for the stock to rebound. You are getting paid while you wait.

You must learn to think contrarily. It's difficult at first because there is so much noise trying to point you in the opposite direction. You must try to become a dispassionate investor. Don't be swayed by daily market movements, pundits, talking heads, people who have something to sell, well-intentioned but clueless friends and relatives, or by your political leanings, for that matter. Be like the aardvark who finds nourishment where no one else thinks to look. Don't be afraid to take advantage of bargains. You do it at the grocery store, the department store, and the automobile dealership (if you're lucky). You most certainly do it every day when you shop online. As an intelligent consumer, you refuse to overpay for something you can get elsewhere for less. Think the same way about shopping for investments. Ignore the noise from people who have their interests—not yours—in mind and trust what you now know to be the truth.

Women Clients

I have a great many women as clients and I enjoy working with them because they tend to be more patient than men and find it easier to think long term. Men, for better or worse, are wired to fix things and quickly. If the market is down, oh my God, I have to sell right away before I am forced to admit I might have made a mistake buying that stock. If a market sector is moving up fast, I have to get in on it so I don't have to admit I missed the boat. As men, we react, whereas women seem better able to analyze data more holistically, evaluating the whole picture from a longer-term perspective.

I think I may have a greater level of compassion than most men. It's possible it is a part of why I was drawn to the priesthood for much of my youth and early adulthood. I've personally experienced the loss of fellow pilots who were friends in the service and came to realize the importance of helping surviving spouses through a terribly difficult time in their lives, making sure the funeral arrangements were properly attended to and just being there for the widow and family members. It's highly unusual for a family to lose their son, husband or father at such a young age. There is no opportunity to say "goodbye" as it typically happens suddenly and without expectation. When you stand next to a widow and hear taps played, then that 21-gun salute roar, it breaks your heart and leaves an indelible moment behind. I can't accurately covey the feeling of hearing the guttural cry of a father who's just lost his son. It's hard for me to think about even now, decades later. That's one reason why I find it so important to be there for my clients as they deal with life's disappointments and tragedies, being able to let them know that at least they will be alright financially. It's a big—and rewarding—part of what I do.

If I Were King

I sometimes think the best form of government would be a noble monarchy or benevolent dictatorship. The problem is that as the proverb goes, "power corrupts; absolute power corrupts absolutely." Thus, I concur with our forefathers that the best alternative is a Republic. Of course, as a monarch, you are in for life so you don't have to worry about pandering to special interests so you can get reelected; you have the ability to simply do what's best for everyone.

If I were that monarch for a day, there are some things I would change about our financial system. First, I would eliminate commissions on the sale of any financial product. The problem with insurance agents, brokers and companies selling you annuities, permanent life insurance and other products you don't need is the high fees and commissions. I would abolish the sale of Wall Street products with commissions, hidden fees and other unwarranted costs to the public. Secondly, I would amend the banking system, bringing back Glass-Steagall separating investment banks from commercial banks. Allowing commercial banks to be intertwined with investment banks creates greater risk to our financial system. No amount of regulation or capitalization can stop the next financial crisis from occurring if these two entities are tied together. As a fee-based advisor, I can, at the very least, avoid many of the conflicts of interest that exist in our industry and better serve private investors.

Our Four Core Pillars

Altrius is founded on four core pillars: Integrity, Compassion, Competence, and Humility. I believe for any business to succeed you must love what you do. You must be honest with your clients. Twenty years of integrity and good work can be eradicated by a single lie by you or any of your associates, who can take down the reputation of the company with one falsehood.

I think being honest with your clients means always being candid, even when it may endanger your business relationship. You must be willing to do that in order to have a mutually beneficial relationship, even if the things you have to say do not initially meet with approval or agreement. A client may not want to hear that if he continues spending at his current rate, he will be out of money long before he is out of retirement, or that by jumping in and out of the market he is doing things that are detrimental to his financial health, but it's my responsibility as trusted advisor to confront clients with reality.

An important business pillar is having confidence in your experience, knowledge and intellectual curiosity. Finance is wonderfully complex and constantly challenging; you have to continually be learning and questioning your beliefs.

No matter how successful, you must have humility. No matter how diligent and dedicated you are to your profession, you will make mistakes. When you do, admit it; take ownership and responsibility for it. Rational, good people understand that no one achieves perfection in this life, everyone makes an occasional mistake. Always question where your investment thesis may be wrong and don't take undue risk through hubris.

Compassion is understanding that life throws curves at everyone and sometimes, the victim of a misfortune needs an empathetic ear. Having gone through a divorce, the death of my father and helping Marines in their time of need have all helped me become more compassionate towards others. Being there for my clients during difficult times—when going through a serious illness or a loved one passes away, or a divorcee fighting for her children—is the most noble aspect of my work and imperative to what we do in our profession.

The success of my firm is also contingent upon convincing our clients to maintain a long-term perspective on their finances. I can assure you that is not the norm for our industry, which is overrun with television pundits, brokers and financial firms driving short-termism.

If you believe in market timing or chasing yield with the expectation of making extraordinary returns, I'm not your guy and Altrius is not the firm for you. If you want someone to tell you the truth, have a passion for what they do, is competent, and has a track record of doing it well for a couple of decades, I might be the right guy for you. I don't take my responsibilities lightly; I know it's your life savings I'm investing for you. I'm investing my life savings alongside you in the same investments as yours.

As a fiduciary, I am ultimately accountable for our clients' assets. The responsibility frequently keeps me up at night, but that goes with the territory. Like everyone, I make mistakes, but I avoid taking too much risk with any single issue or deviating from our core principles. I attempt to avoid the large mistakes many on Wall Street make by using leverage to chase yield or concentration to pursue extraordinary returns.

I'm more than proud that our clients have adopted our long-term orientation, embraced our three-pronged strategy of investing like an aardvark, and given me the privilege of serving as their trusted advisor. I hope to continue to do so for many decades to come.

Endnotes

[1] Karen Dolan, "Announcing the Morningstar Fund Managers of the Decade," <u>Morningstar Fund Spy</u> 12 Jan 2010.

[2] "A Brief history of Behavioral Finance," finworx.com 11 Aug 2016.

[3] Globoforce.com

[4] John Nofsinger, "Surprised Again? The Anchoring Bias of Investors," <u>Psychology Today</u> 21 Jul 2008.

[5] Chris Baysden, "Gillings' group buys Quintiles for $1.7B, will take it private," bizjournals.com 11 Apr 2003.

[6] investopedia

[7] Kendra Cherry, "What is a Confirmation Bias?" Cognitive Psychology, verywell.com 21 Aug 2017.

[8] usnews.com

[9] quora.com

[10] Brad M Barber and Terrance Odean, "Trading Is Hazardous to Your Wealth: The Common Stock Investment Performance of Individual Investors," <u>The Journal of Finance</u> Apr 2000.

[11] Don Phillips, "Alternative Funds Are in a Time Warp," morningstar.com 02 Feb 2018.

[12] Chris Flood, "Global shift into alternative assets gathers pace," <u>Financial Times</u> 16 July 2017.

[13] Sarah Max, "Alternative Investments: Surfing the Market," <u>Barron's</u> 24 Oct 2015.

[14] A covered call is an options strategy whereby an investor holds a long position in an asset and writes (sells) call options on that asset in an attempt to generate increased income.

[15] usatoday.com

[16] Burton Malkiel, "Investors' Most Serious Mistakes," wealthfront.com 02 Feb 2013.

[17] Investopedia.com

[18] Absolute return funds tend to take short positions and use derivatives to achieve returns.

[19] Wikipedia.org.

[20] "Warren Buffett on using leverage to invest," usatoday.com 19 Jan 2014.

[21] www.investopedia.com/articles/economics/09/lehman-brothers-collapse.asp.

[22] www.princeton.edu/ceps/workingpapers/124malkiel.pdf.

[23] Hema Parmar, Katia Porzecanski and Katherine Nurton, "John Paulson's Merger Arbitrage Fund Plunged at the Start of the Year," Bloomberg LP 19 Mar 2018.

[24] Akin Oyedele, "Warren Buffett offers his 'strongest argument' against a practice investors are doing in record numbers," <u>Business Insider</u> 27 Feb 2018.

[25] Mike Skrobin, "The Evolution of Television News," <u>Watercooler Journal</u> 5 Aug 2015.

[26] Paul C Tetlock, "Giving Content to Investor Sentiment: The Role of Media in the Stock Market," <u>Journal of Finance</u> 8 May 2007.

[27] Gordon Clark, Nigel Thrift & Adam Tickell, "Performing finance: the industry, the media and its image, <u>Review of International Political Economy</u> 04 June 2010.

[28] Ivestopedia.com

[29] Jack Gray, "Misadventures of an Irresponsible Investor," <u>Pension Management</u> Fall 2012.

[30] Larry Swedroe, "The Issues with Socially Responsible Investing," Moneywatch-cbsnews.com 20 Sep 2011.

[31] Keith Evans, "What Are the Disadvantages of Corporate Social Responsibility?" bizfluent.com 26 Sep 2017.

[32] http://knowyourmeme.com/memes/once-ler

[33] "Let Us Prey: How Church Scam Artists Get Away With Millions," scambusters.org

[34] "Affinity Fraud: How to Avoid Investment Scams That Target Groups," sec.gov 9 Oct 2013.

[35] Ibid.

[36] Louis K C Chan and Josef Lakonishok, "Growth Investing: Review and Update," <u>Financial Analysts Journal</u> 2004.

[37] Wikipedia.org

[38] Richard Oppel Jr, "Conservative Fidelity Fund Manager Resigns," <u>New York Times</u> 13 Jan 2000.

[39] Beth Healy, "Five things you should know about Karen Firestone," <u>Boston Globe</u> 22 May 2016.

[40] Franco Modigliani and Merton Miller, "The Cost of Capital, Corporation Finance and the Theory of Investment", <u>The American Economic Review</u>, 1958.

[41] Douglas J. Skinner and Eugene Soltes, "What do dividends tell us about earnings quality?" 2009.

[42] Malcolm Baker, Brock Mendel and Jeffrey Wurgler, "Dividends as Reference Points: A Behavioral Signaling Approach," 22 Jan 2015.

[43] Eugene F. Fama and Kenneth R. French, "Disappearing Dividends: Changing Firm Characteristics or Lower Propensity to Pay?" 2000.

[44] Malcolm Baker and Jeffrey Wurgler, "A Catering Theory of Dividends," <u>Journal of Finance</u> 2004.

[45] King Fuei Lee, "Demographics, Dividend Clienteles and the Dividend Premium," <u>The Quarterly Review of Economics and Finance</u>, Dec 2010.

[46] Investopedia.com

[47] financial-dictionary.com

[48] Investopedia.com

[49] dividendinvestor.com

[50] Leslie Kramer, "It's high time for a blunt conversation about investing and market crashes," cnbc.com 13 Mar 2017.

[51] Steven Overly, "Americans bought more cars than ever last year. In 2017, things could get bumpy." Washington Post 4 Jan 2017.

[52] Statista.com

[53] Robin Chase, "Car-sharing Offers Convenience, Saves Money and Helps the Environment," YouAsked@state.gov.

[54] Chris Isadore, "GM sells 10 million cars for first time thanks to China," money.cnn.com 7 Feb 2017.

[55] A black swan is an event or occurrence that deviates beyond what is normally expected of a situation and is extremely difficult to predict. Black swan events are typically random and unexpected. (Investopedia)

[56] Andrew Ellul, Chotibhak Jotikasthira, and Christian T. Lundblad, "Regulatory Pressure and Fire Sales in the Corporate Bond Market," Oct 2010.

[57] The legislation of 1933 contained four provisions that separated commercial and investment banking. Starting in the early 1960s, federal banking regulators' interpretations of the Act permitted commercial banks and their affiliates to engage in an expanding list and volume of securities activities. Ultimately, the 1999 Gramm-Leach-Bliley Act (GLBA) repealed the two provisions restricting affiliations between banks and securities firms. By that time, many commentators argued Glass–Steagall was already "dead". Most notably, Citibank's 1998 affiliation with Salomon Smith Barney, one of the largest US securities firms, was permitted under the FED's then existing interpretation of the Glass–Steagall Act. In November 1999, President Bill Clinton publicly declared "the Glass–Steagall law is no longer appropriate."

[58] Zachary Karabell, "The Shame of the Ratings Agencies: How Moody's Blows It Again," Time 03 June 2011.

[59] "Competency, Trustworthiness of Ratings, and Conflicts of Interest," Brotman Law

[60] CFR Staff, "The Credit Rating Controversy," Council on Foreign Relations 19 Feb 2015.

[61] Investopedia.com

[62] ssa.gov

[63] Investopedia.com.

[64] Ashlea Eberling, "Final Tax Bill Includes Huge Estate Tax Win For The Rich: The $22.4 Million Exemption," Forbes 21 Dec 2017.

[65] Investopedia.com

[66] thebalance.com

[67] Investopedia.com

[68] thebalance.com

[69] celebritynetworth.com

[70] www.sec.gov/litigation/complaints/comp18090.htm

[71] Steve Kroft, "State Budgets: Day of Reckoning," CBS 60 Minutes, 9 Dec 2010.

[72] The procedure whereby an issuer designs a financial instrument merging various financial assets and then markets tiers of the repackaged instruments to investors. (Wikipedia)

[73] Value at risk is a measure of the risk of loss for investments. It estimates how much a set of investments might lose, given normal market conditions, in a set time period. (Investopedia)

[74] ibid

CPSIA information can be obtained
at www.ICGtesting.com
Printed in the USA
BVHW042058140319
541884BV00009B/17/P